DIVORCE *drinking* & DATING

THE NO-FAIL PROCESS TO FIND OUT WHO YOU REALLY ARE
FIND YOUR OWN FREEDOM
AND HAVE A FEW LAUGHS ALONG THE WAY

Danielle Prahl

Publishing Services provided by Paper Raven Books

Printed in the United States of America

First Printing, 2017

Paperback = 978-0-9996206-1-8
Hardback = 978-0-9996206-0-1

To Vail: You are the greatest gift I have ever received. I hope you always have the courage to follow your passions with reckless abandon. May you always be surrounded with endless love and support, and have a heart full of joy.

To Mom: Thank you for always believing in me. You are love.

And last but not least — to the Woman inside of you who longs for freedom, too: I give you permission to have, do, and be ANYTHING that you want on this earth.

Table of Contents

Introduction   1

Part 1:

Chapter 1: **What. The. F*ck.**   7
Chapter 2: **The Story of Me**   13
Chapter 3: **Our Love Story**   19
Chapter 4: **My Own Little Fairytale**   47
Chapter 5: **How to Help Someone Destroy
Your Self-Worth**   51
Chapter 6: **Nobody Envies Your Life. In Fact, Your
Family and Friends Think Your Life Is Way More
Messed Up than You Do**   61
Chapter 7: **Everybody Else Knows What's Best for You**   65
Chapter 8: **You're Moving Down in the World
(and Fast)**   69
Chapter 9: **You Aren't Doing Misery Correctly**   75

Part 2:

Chapter 10: **The Best Way to Get over Someone Is to
Date Pretty Much Anyone Else**   81
Chapter 11: **Just When You Think You Have
Hit Rock Bottom, Grab a Shovel**   85
Chapter 12: **The Minute You Are Uncoupling,
Everyone Else Is Coupling**   99

Chapter 13: **How to Date a Crackhead and Other Stories** 105

Chapter 14: **The Grass Isn't Always Greener, but It's Still Freakin Grass** 113

Chapter 15: **How to Convince Your Parents You Are Suicidal and Date Your Ex's Friends** 117

Chapter 16: **The $200,000 Baby** 123

Chapter 17: **Birthday Boy** 131

Chapter 18: **How to Burn Your Old Life Down** 141

Part 3:

Chapter 19: **Two Years Later** 155

Chapter 20: **Opening the Flood Gates at My Best Friend's F*cked Up Wedding** 173

Part 4:

Chapter 21: **A New Perspective** 185

Chapter 22: **Making Money is GOOD** 193

Chapter 23: **Women Are the Most Powerful Creatures on the Planet** 201

Chapter 24: **Why Figuring Out Who You Are Is Bullsh*t** 207

Chapter 25: **Time Does Not Heal All Wounds You Gotta Do the Work** 211

Chapter 26: **Happy Endings? (We're Not at a Massage Parlor)** 219

Introduction

For the woman inside of you who longs for freedom.

*Y*ou know those perfect people who never complain about their partner, always have their shit together, and do the right thing? Yeah, that's not me. I'm more the type of person who tells my best friend that I want to murder my spouse when he keeps me up snoring, that I want to trip the old person walking too slowly in front of me, and that I want to yell at that lady's unruly child who won't stop screaming inside the supermarket. I also have a ton of compassion, a huge heart, and a giving spirit. I guess what I'm trying to say is, I can be a bit complicated. I bet you feel me on that one. Am I right?

Life is complicated. Relationships change everything. No one prepares you for major events like marriage, divorce, dating, or having kids. Why does no one talk about these incredibly important parts of life? Well, I think it's time we all started being honest about some of the crazy stories we've lived through. Tell you what, I'll go first, and then I'll invite you to get honest about your life, too.

Because of some deep-rooted beliefs and how I valued myself, I entered into a relationship that ended up turning my life upside down. Through hard work, self-discovery, coaching, lots of books, and other steps I'll talk about, I took an experience that could have devastated me and used it to launch myself into a life I couldn't even have dreamed of. I want to share that with you so you can find the courage to create a better life for yourself (you know, the kind you really want).

I can't promise that this book will change your life. Or that even after reading it you will know everything and be on your way to miraculous riches, the best relationships ever, and life in a mansion in the Swiss Alps, or whatever. I can promise that this book is brutally honest, raw, the vast majority of it was written in the moment from my perspective and thoughts at that time. Yes, this is a true story, not embellished for Hollywood-like drama.

In the span of a year and a half, I went from completely destroying my life—living at my mom's house with no job and a bunch of debt, and having a conman ex-husband with a jail sentence—to accomplishing the following:

- Experiencing true joy and bliss again.

- Starting the journey of becoming a mom (and later providing a great life for my daughter).

- Earning six-figures from a business, working for myself from home.

- Buying myself a brand-new car.

- Living in my dream location a stone's throw from the beach.

- Finding my purpose for right now, by helping women like you to design true success in their businesses and lives.

And I did all of that without borrowing money, begging on the streets, or even starting a GoFundMe page.

Incredible, right? WRONG. These are minuscule things in the grand scheme of life.

I am capable of so much more and you are, too, my friend. You can truly be, do, and have *anything* in this world. You are not a mistake. Maybe you've lived through something similar to what I'm about to share with you in this book. Maybe you've experienced something even crazier. Either way, we are strong, we are resilient. There's nothing we can't live through and be better on the other side for it.

In doing the work to learn about myself, who I am and what I want; I was able to crawl out of the shambles. But you shouldn't have to. I would be so much further along without these mistakes, if I'd had the tools in my belt that I do now prior to this disaster happening. Everything happens for a reason, and I truly believe that this happened to me for a purpose: to share my story with you. All of it. The good, the bad, the embarrassing, and the ugly.

I hope that you take something from this book, that my suffering, my crazy and wild stories, my heartbreaks and victories, will leave you with some wisdom or nuggets that you can use for yourself. Take what you can from all of it, and go create the life you truly want.

Together, powerful women are going to change this world.

Part 1:
The Fall

Chapter 1:
What. The. F*ck.

*L*et me start by saying this is my story from my perspective. It's not about my ex-husband, the other people involved, or anyone else. It is about me; a 20-something newlywed, who spent six years dating, one year married, to a man who disappeared overnight. Well, disappeared isn't really the word I am looking for. How about incarcerated? Locked up. In the pokey. You get it. What follows are my thoughts written down at the time the events occurred. With the passage of time, I've had more insight into these events and I've recorded those thoughts, too.

May 21, 2015

My world crumbled overnight. Last night, in fact. We were married. I thought he was a good person. I figured it was like a bad blast from the past coming back to haunt him. So, I won't lie and say I was completely blindsided. I mean, unless you call being blindsided thinking that he was at a business meeting and then finding out that he was literally being extradited from California to Texas. He spent a bunch of our savings without asking or telling me. He subsequently hired then fired more attorneys than Mariah Carey does assistants. Now I know what you're thinking: what an idiot this chick is (me, not Mariah). But just hear me out. I didn't know about any of this before.

We had some excellent years together before this. But he wasn't honest with me about the situation.

He lied through his teeth and told me nonsense. He wore me down whenever I tried asking questions. If I thought something was fishy, he made me feel like the cray-cray one. Being Glenda the Dumb Witch, I stuck in there. I believed the things he told me. He told me this was all a big mistake. He did some business deals that apparently weren't so above-board. Of course, that's not according to him; obviously, he was a little angel. I'm not an attorney, but I'm also not an idiot. So, SEVEN years later when we were newly married and building a life together, the state of Texas turned around and leveled his entire life harder than Miley Cyrus's wrecking ball. And my life, too.

So, here's what happened. Yesterday, my husband flew to Texas. According to him, he was going to a "business meeting." Something didn't feel right, but we were having problems in our marriage and I was so emotionally exhausted that I really didn't even care. It was a relief to have him gone. I went for the night to stay with one of my BFFs in LA, because I had an appointment the next day in the area. I got a text from him this morning: "I was sentenced to prison. I'm sorry. I love you. Call my mom."

I almost threw up in my mouth. Maybe it was a joke? It's not April Fool's Day, but something inside me sunk. I knew it was true. It's like when you're in a car crash, and you can see it happening in slow motion. I had just left my friend's house and was driving to my appointment like it was a normal Thursday morning. I read the text, had a meltdown, looked out the window to see some bitches sipping their Coffee Bean like nothing bad was happening in the world. Assholes.

I called his mom, and she said, "Yeah, well, maybe we can appeal and we will see."

Me: "So what exactly happened?"

Her: "Well, you know, he was really upset, and they thought he may need suicide watch, and I don't know, I tried to tell him maybe he will only serve a few years."

Me: "Okay, wait. What is going on???"

Her: "Well, the prosecution requested he get 20 years 'cause he posts pictures on social media like he's out with movie stars and stuff."

Side note: Umm, we live in LA. The movie star is sometimes our waiter. I found out later that the prosecutor also mentioned a photo of him on Facebook in a Ferrari, "proving" he clearly has the money and is just choosing not to pay it back. The photo mentioned was my husband taking my stepdad for a ride in his friend's Ferrari. My stepdad had never been in one and H (my husband) took him around the block in it. I posted a picture for my stepdad on his Facebook. I guess that's what you call a lavish lifestyle, as well as "evidence" in the state of Texas. Also, H was dumb and wanted everyone to think he was awesome.

(Back to the conversation)

Me: "Hello! How long was he sentenced?!?!?!?!? And for what??????"

Her: "Fourteen years. And he has to pay back the money when he gets out."

Drop the mic.

Fourteen years??? I literally was supposed to pick him up from the airport a few hours later. I had no clue. And money??? What money?

Did he have a clue? Maybe. He was acting out in our relationship recently. He even contacted an ex-girlfriend that I'm pretty sure he slept with, and I caught him texting some other girls. And a prostitute. And I found him on Tinder. You know, normal marriage stuff. As if standing by your man for a felony conviction, you didn't know about, doesn't make you feel stupid enough; having him cheat on you during the WHOLE situation helps.... And somehow him being so fucked up mentally that YOU feel bad for his situation is, like, a certain special type of brilliance. Who am I? He also got a mercy tattoo, against my objections, of my name. Tattooed. On his chest. His only tattoo. Talk about emotional terrorism.

Moral of the story: maybe he knew more than I did about the impending issue. After a year of dealing with his destructive ways every month, in a brand-new marriage, is pretty much when most people would just take some Xanax and turn into a vegetable or move to Guam. I stayed right where I was, in hopes that this was like some bad weather that would blow over and settle, and life would resume.

Now I have been sitting here all day literally doing stuff like Googling "What to do with your husband's shit while he is in jail" and "What happens to an incarcerated person's bills?" There is no *Things to Do While Your Husband Is at the Farm for Dummies.* When people are down and bleeding, that is when the wolves really come out. Will divorcing him immediately protect me from further lawsuits that he may have somehow gotten in to? Did I even know this person? Did I need to pay off his bills so he isn't more screwed when he gets out some day?

With all the money he *didn't* leave me, that isn't an option. The best part of being with someone who lies to you repeatedly, is when they spend all your community property cash like it's the last money on earth and leave you with nothing. Not to mention you have their lifetime of accumulated belongings sitting in every corner of your home together as a reminder. I mean, where do I send his clothes? His shoes are still by the door like he is going to come home any minute and be like, "Got ya! Wasn't this the best joke ever?"

So, I am texting my friends, who are all out, either partying happily or planning for their new babies or their weddings. But I am here; listing my husband's shit on eBay, hoping that I can pay down the bills and find an apartment that isn't cockroach-infested. (I have lived with the cockroaches before, my friend, and I am not going back to that.) And now eBay has some dumb rule where you can only list a certain amount of stuff per month. The rest, I guess, I'll have to get rid of on Craigslist. Is there a store called We Buy Your Shit, and they just pay you for some of the nice shit you have? What do I do with his car? I remember when my largest problem was what outfit to wear out with my friends.

The sad part is that I thought he was such a dream. He was funny, charismatic, good-looking, charming, and kind-hearted. When he wasn't pissing me off, he was even really fun. And man did we have fun. He could also be extremely giving. Even when we were hurting for money, he would buy other people's dinner if they were having a hard time. He would help anyone in need, and he never asked for anything in return.

Now, in hindsight, I realize it was probably guilt kindness. Making up for passed fucked-upness. Giving away your money all the time and having no boundaries is not going to bring you what you want. If you are being generous and paying for things because you think you should, but really it makes you feel like shit inside, you are going to have some problems.

So, yeah, it sucks. Yes, it feels unjust. Did he deserve "14-years-in-jail" fuck up? I don't know. The weirdest part about not being able to say goodbye and having him hauled off to jail, is I feel like he was either a) a dream that I made up and he was never here, and now I just get to pack up his shit as punishment for dreaming so long. Or, b) he died.

I literally am mourning the loss of a life I was building with someone, who was taken from me overnight, and for the life of me I can't figure out why. Sure, on paper, I get it. Actually, not really. That court jargon shit makes zero sense. Have you ever heard of "misappropriation of fiduciary responsibility?" Yeah, me neither. It would have been helpful if he were more upfront, obviously. At times he was too optimistic, to the point where he didn't take things as seriously as he should have. Maybe he was lying to himself. He clearly lied to me. But, like, cosmically and religiously, when it comes to his life now, when it comes to my life now... What. The. FUCK.

Chapter 2:
The Story of Me

It's hard to comprehend the gravity and the depth of what other people are going through until you have experienced true loss. Devastation. Mourning. Hurting. Pain. People these days can be summed up by what they post about their lives on Instagram (and we take that for complete realness now). My social media highlight reel used to be poppin', I'll tell you that much. Yet, in order for you to get how I ended up here, in the present moment, maybe I should go back to where it all began.

I grew up in a small town in Laramie, Wyoming. People call it "God's country," beautiful or homegrown America. I couldn't wait to leave this place, even when it was the only place I knew. As a little girl, I watched movies and read books about people in cities with opportunities and jobs, living lives I had never fathomed before. I had a deep-rooted sense of adventure, and I couldn't wait to get out of the town that isolated me, from what I thought was "real," and stat experiencing the rest of what the world had to offer. I guess I saw it in a movie or something. I decided very early on that the place for me would be California, and I would move there as soon as physically possible.

One of my best friends growing up, Terri, was from out of town. Her family moved to Laramie, and she joined my third-grade class at the beginning of the year. She had jet black hair and wore tie-dye clothes, which was unlike anything I had ever seen. Terri's family was different than mine and different from the rest of the people in town, and I loved every second of that. They all had dark-colored hair and eyes, and fair skin that almost made them look like they had perpetual bags under their eyes, making them seem even more mysterious.

Terri and I became fast friends. I spent many a night over at their house listening to the stories of the places they had visited and learning about her mom's journey as an artist. They had a garage sale once, and they graciously gave me a Katherine Hepburn autobiography on audio tape and a gold kimono. I had no clue what a kimono was at the time; I just thought it was a really cool bathrobe that rich people wore, and I often threw it on in the mornings when it was cold, to eat breakfast in before school.

Little did I know that the garage sale was a preamble to them moving away. After a *South Park* marathon on a snowy Saturday, Terri spilled to me that they would shortly be moving to Sacramento, California. I was devastated. It seemed again that California was haunting me. We made plans that I would take a bus to see her after she moved (because a plane was too expensive and a bus just seemed more logical), but neither of us realized that they didn't allow third graders to travel via bus alone, and that my allowance money wouldn't get me to the bus station, let alone halfway across the country.

My mom was a sheriff deputy, and one of her cases happened to be a murder case that gained national attention. A young man named Matthew Shepard was beaten to death, not far outside of the city limits of our little town. I remember finding some paperwork about it, one early morning, on our kitchen table. My mom must have been up late, because she forgot to put it up. It wasn't anything spectacular or serious, but I do remember seeing Matthew Shepard's name on the paper and not thinking much of it. It was 1998, and Matthew ended up dying. I was 11 years old.

This caused a lot of serious heartache for many people connected to the case, not only his family, but also his friends and our town. It was like dropping a pebble in a puddle of water; it simply rippled out from there. Matt was HIV-positive, and my mom, being the first person to respond to the scene, was giving him CPR trying to save his life. The department she worked for had ordered cheaper gloves than usual that kept breaking, and, in her high-pressure situation, she ran out and went ahead with CPR anyway. I like to think that this act bought Matthew a few more days on this earth. They may not have been conscious ones or the time you would hope for, but enough time for his family to be able to come and be with him before he passed.

Unfortunately, my mom was exposed to HIV when she tried to save him, as she had cuts all over her hands from building a lean-to for our llamas. (I tried to tell you we were country folk that lived in the middle of nowhere.) She had to be put on AZT drugs and would be tested months down the line to make sure she had not contracted it. During this time, I remember her being scared, afraid to touch us, afraid of what may happen. She was sick all of the time, vomiting, her hair falling out. She couldn't work even though she loved her job, as she spent most her time in the upstairs bedroom on the floor near the toilet.

My stepdad was now granted the glorious job of caring for three girls who did their best to give him a run for his money. I even blew up a casserole dish once while trying to make mac and cheese with my friend. I didn't know casserole dishes couldn't go on the stove top. I just thought it was a "pretty dish," and didn't know why we never used this to cook in on the stove. Now I know.

While she was dealing with the misery of being poisoned at the cellular level to hopefully save her life, the case garnered national attention, and the media was all over it. There were many aspects to the case that people were interested in. For one, Matthew was openly gay (and I don't care what anyone said, that was not the norm in our town at the time), plus it was starting to come out about his HIV, among other things. My mom now had to deal with being sick from the medication, as well as getting calls from the media, people questioning how she could be so stupid as to risk her life to save a "gay," or praising her as a hero. It was a strange dichotomy and a stressful time for us, yet I can't imagine what Matthew's family must have been going through at the time.

A doctor in Denver heard about my mom's story and offered to pay for her to get some sort of advanced early blood screening to make sure that she didn't contract HIV, so that she could stop the drugs early and continue her life. It was truly a blessing. I was too young to remember his name now, but wherever you are, sir, we are in a great deal of debt to you. She hated taking those drugs, and we could finally find out one way or the other the fate of my mom's health and life. I am happy to say that her test came back negative for HIV, and it seemed that life could resume for us as normal. Yet, normal it was not.

A theater company wanted to make a play out of the story and ended up visiting our home. It was the first time I had met actual people who were actors, writers, and directors for their real full-time jobs. I was fascinated by these people from New York and asked them question after question when they came to our house to interview my mom. My mom didn't really want to talk to anyone at the time, but I guess they had gotten in touch with her and, with encouragement from my grandma, there was something about them that made her feel their intentions were in the right place.

I was late to the party, because nobody told me that they were coming. I had been out doing early trick-or-treating with a friend and walked into our living room dressed as a dead bride with fake blood all over me, to find a bunch of well-dressed New Yorkers in our house. I loved them immediately. I wanted to be an actress at that age, and I'm sure I bothered them incessantly about everything I possibly could.

The play they wrote went on to be *The Laramie Project,* which is still being performed all over the world. HBO later decided to make a movie out of it, and because my mom was a character portrayed, she was invited to Los Angeles for the press conference that year for all of HBO's upcoming shows. My mom hates the press, doesn't like to talk to strangers, and is an extremely private person. Her immediate instinct was to say no, but I caught wind of it and all I heard was California, so I begged her to go and bring me with her.

After much back and forth, she decided to go (I know wholeheartedly it was mostly for me) and somehow convinced them to allow me to come with her and my stepdad. We would be making the trek out to Pasadena, California to the Ritz Carlton for the press conference, and my mom would be speaking as a panel member. I can recount so many things about that trip: how at age 13, I flew first class and rode in a limo for the first time, how

I got to meet Monica Lewinsky, how Alec Baldwin taught me how to take a selfie (before selfies were even a thing), and how I got to sit at a table with the head of HBO and eat fancy food I couldn't pronounce the names of.

What really stuck out to me about that trip, though, was a feeling that I would never forget. As I sat in my hotel room and looked out the window at the lights of Los Angeles beyond us, all I felt was magic. These sparkling lights of the skyline at night pumped something into my veins that felt like pure opportunity, excitement, and yet somehow also felt like home. This experience cemented in me that I could do and be and have anything I wanted in life, and that California was where I was meant to be. I could barely sleep the rest of the trip and sat up for hours with the radio on, looking out at those lights, dreaming of the woman who I would become living in this beautiful place.

Chapter 3:
Our Love Story

I moved from Laramie to Denver, Colorado pretty much as soon as possible after high school. After I finished up some courses at the University of Wyoming, I headed to Denver and enrolled in hair school. Going to hair school full time was extremely hard, and I balanced it with working an additional 40 hours a week as a waitress at night, with doubles on my "days off."

Why Hair? Why Denver? Denver was the closest "big city" near to my small town. That and everyone told me I was nuts and would never make it in California, it seemed like a safe enough in-between to see if I could survive. Being a good two hours from home and experiencing a taste of the city life was great; the problem was that I didn't want to follow a traditional career track in corporate America. I just felt there was something much, much larger that I could do. Growing up, I always had a strangely close bond with my hairstylists, and being a stylist seemed to offer the opportunity to be creative and to work for myself. I didn't know quite what it was I was called to do yet, but helping women feel good about themselves and being my own boss seemed kind of on the right track, so hair school it was. I was a large proponent of self-help and working on my mindset long before that was a buzz word.

When I was in hair school, living in a studio apartment with a bed to my name and a computer I bought for $100, my mom sent me a copy of Eckhart Tolle's *A New Earth*. Before that I fell in love with Jack Canfield's success principles. Marianne Williamson's *A Woman's Worth* is still to this day one of my favorite gifts to give to women I connect with, who seem to be at a low point when I know their highs have SO high to go. I've always envisioned a life much bigger than the one I currently had.

After completing the 1800-hour cosmetology program and passing my licensing exam, I sublet my downtown Denver apartment and decided to head home for three months (to save money before I finally made the trek to California). I got my old job back from high school and moved back in with good ol' mom. Even though it seemed like one step forward, two steps back, I knew ultimately it would allow me to leap ahead.

Everyone told me I would fail (except my ever-encouraging parents of course, even though they weren't thrilled), but I packed all the clothes I owned into the backseat of my Ford Mustang and drove straight through to California. Initially, I stayed with the one person I knew in the area from my hometown, who had graduated years earlier. He lived about an hour outside of LA and while that would be a bit of a trick, he was gracious enough to let me live rent-free until I found my own place. Due to sheer perseverance and lady balls, I landed a job at a super high-end salon and found a shithole place to live within three months. (For real shithole, as in a room in damn near South Central that had bugs in it. Gotta start somewhere, right? Welcome to Hollywood, what's your dream?)

It was a fateful night in Hollywood the evening I met H, the man who would later become my husband. By this time, I was living in the up-and-coming neighborhood of Koreatown and spent most of my time at work. To celebrate a coworker's fiancé's birthday, we all went to a nightclub called Echo. I was basically the 13th wheel in a group full of couples, so I had a few drinks, meandered around making friends, and made my way to the dance floor.

The next thing I knew, a tall and strikingly handsome man grabbed my arm and, beneath his low tipped baseball cap, said to me, "Hey, want a drink?" Of course, I said yes. We were at the bar waiting to get our drinks when it seemed this guy knew everyone in the place. I believe he introduced himself at some point, but I was not exactly listening. The lady bartender knew this mystery man as well and handed us shots across the bar for no reason (Patrón, which I don't care for, but hey, free drinks).

We were dancing and having fun, caught up in our own little world. This guy asked me for my number, and I handed him my phone. We chatted a bit but not about anything important. To be fair he wasn't particularly my type, but I hadn't really been on a date or met anyone I liked much, even though I'd been in California for some time now. All I really did was work, work more, work some more, attend stand-up comedy classes, and go on hikes or to the beach. That was my life. I looked around and realized that my friends were no longer at their table or on the dancefloor for that matter. I tried calling one of them and was informed they had made their way back to the hotel, which meant I had been left at Echo. It wasn't too far, so it wasn't the end of the world, but I decided it was time to call it a night as well.

Somehow, mystery man, whose name turned out to be "H," convinced me to let him drive me home, as his car was across the street and I didn't live very far. This was not normally something I would ever agree to, but he somehow convinced me that this was a totally reasonable idea. I had my keys between my knuckles for safety and 911 on speed dial, so I guess as a 21-year-old girl in a huge city, it seemed fine.

We walked over to the parking garage and climbed in his Range Rover. I was sitting in the passenger seat when two more guys climbed in the back, "Hey, H, can you drive us to Studio City real quick?" H told them no at first, but eventually they wore him down, and he asked if I was cool to take a quick drive. My home was a few minutes away, and Studio City was not. There was no way in hello I was going to Studio city "real quick" with these people, and wasn't even convinced taking a ride to my house was a great idea. Now, I'm not great at math or anything, but I was counting the number of men in the car in comparison to me and something didn't add up. I swiftly hopped out of the car, chucked him the peace sign behind me and scurried out of there. One short cab ride later, I was safe at home.

The next morning, I awoke to a text message of H's abs with an accompanying text, "This is what you missed out on last night." I responded with a screenshot from the Internet of a girl tied up in a basement and say, "No, actually, this is probably more what I missed out on last night." You know, given the awkward circumstances we left on. He sent that text at around 3 AM, so I dismissed it as a drunk text and got on with my day.

Over the next several days, H reached out to me pretty regularly. We had good banter back and forth, He didn't shy away from my sadistic humor responses and actually seemed to have a decent sense of humor himself. He asked me out quite a few times, and I more or less brushed the subject under the rug. Truthfully, he wasn't really my type. Sure, he was good-looking (from what I remember, it was dark and he was in a hat for Christ's sake), but physically he was different from most people that I've dated. I could get over that, but more unforgivably, he seemed to think highly of himself.

Late one night, my mom called while my roommate at the time was out (she was never really home), and I was telling my mom about how lonely I had been. Sure, I had made some amazing friends in LA and was always working, but I wished I could meet someone to date, have fun with, maybe make-out with once in a while. I almost felt like a prisoner who hadn't had any sort of human contact in ages. Getting my hair washed at work was really the only time I had another human touch me, as people aren't really touchy feely in LA. Living in a major city can be weird that way at times, being constantly surrounded by people yet feeling so alone, especially as a new person in town without familiar faces to run into. Even a random friendly hug would be nice. As warm as it was outside, it felt...*cold.*

"You said you met a guy a few weeks ago that keeps inviting you out, why don't you just go out with him?" My mom brought it up in a fashion that only mothers can.

"Yeah, I know Mom, but he just isn't my type."

"Isn't your type how?"

"He just isn't. I can't really explain it."

"Well I'm sick of hearing you complain that you are lonely. Someone is adamantly asking you out, just go! Hell, if nothing else you'll get a free dinner! Have a little fun."

I decided she was right. The next time H asked me out, I would accept his invitation. Two days later at work, I got a text from him inviting me to dinner (because, you know, people only text these days and have lost the ability to make an actual phone call). I told him I couldn't that night, but I'd be happy to the next night on Saturday, if he was around. I wasn't a last minute date type; either he would take 24 hours to wait and put some shit together, or he sucked at life and we weren't going out at all. He said tomorrow was great. The next day, we had our usual banter about absolutely nothing, and H informed me that we were going to dinner around 8 PM that night. "So, what time should I pick you up?" he asked.

"Umm, no thanks. I'll drive." I couldn't get my possible kidnapping in his car last time out of my head. Plus, it just didn't really seem safe. I know that was all gentlemanly and such, but I'd rather have my own car and be able to leave when I wanted.

"Alright, fine, you can park in my parking garage, I'll text you the location."

"Can't you just tell me the address of the restaurant? I'd rather meet you there…" This started to make me feel paranoid.

"LOL you are really on one, aren't you? Listen I'm not trying to trap you or something. Since you won't let me pick you up, you can park in my parking garage at my building. It's free. There's a visitor's area and you can come and go when you want. The restaurant is across the street but street parking is horrible and your only other option is expensive valet."

Well, shit.

A few hours later he texted me again, "Hey cutie, send me a pic." Ugh. I loathed this text message more than anything on this earth. If I wanted you to have a picture of me, you would have one. That would be because we had actually spent time together or knew one another. The only thing guys use pictures for is their weird mental fantasies, to ask their friends' opinions, or to brag later on. No thanks.

I sent back a picture of the creepy guy on the tricycle in a mask from the Saw movie. "No for real," he responded, unamused. "Send me a picture…"

"Why, you forgot what I looked like already? That's okay. I forgot what you looked like, too." Which was true, I really couldn't quite remember at this point what the guy looked like. Sure, I remember thinking he was attractive, but it was dark, I was drunk, and his hat was covering most of his face.

That text seemed to shut him up. As I arrived per the instructions at his building, I pulled into what appeared to be a Bed Bath & Beyond parking structure and found an empty spot. I headed toward the elevator to find an attractive man standing by the exit the doors. I immediately recognized it was him. He gave me a hug and made funny comments, and I felt at ease immediately. I was nervous beforehand about the date, the logistics, all of that stuff, but that melted away the moment we met up.

That night ended up being one of the most fun dates I had ever been on. We ate at Katana, a sushi restaurant overlooking Sunset Boulevard that had a balcony dimly lit by string lights. I couldn't afford shit like that at the time, so it was a treat for me. Again, everyone there seemed to know him. We got the best seat and amazing service, and I was embarrassed to tell him I knew jack about sushi, so I told him just to order and surprise me. Dudes like taking the lead and stuff like that anyway, right?

We talked as if we had known each other for a long time. After dinner and a few cocktails, the night was still young and he asked if I wanted to go a nightclub and do some dancing. Umm, yes?! Sometimes it sucks to go to nightclubs with guys. Okay, almost always. You have to wait outside in line, the people in line always give the guys a hard time, and it's just easier if you are a girl to go with other girls. This time was different though. We walked past the packed line outside at a hotspot I had been wanting to go to. The guy at the door knew him and opened the velvet rope for us like Moses parting the red sea. The place was called Voyeur, and I immediately understood why. The inside was dark and saucy, and women in lingerie crawled on a rope net in the ceiling above you. It seemed very sultry and fun. We danced and laughed, and he really made me feel like I could be myself and let my hair down. The rest of the world simply stopped moving around us that night.

A few days later, we went for a hike together in Runyon Canyon, and he asked me what I wanted to do with my life. I wanted to write a book, to own my own business of some sort, and to travel the world. I wanted to be a successful woman and to make a real difference. I just couldn't see the exact path of how to do it yet. He was truly easy to talk to and encouraged me, that all of these things were actually possible. Where I grew up, people normally laughed at people saying things like this. Most of the people I grew up with graduated high school, went to college, got a job, and waited for a promotion. Sure, it was fun to dream, but to have someone who seemed to actually be successful on their own terms telling me that they understood my vision for my life and wholeheartedly believed that would be a reality, well, that blew my mind. I suddenly started to take him a bit more seriously.

The only real issue I had with H was that he was clearly a cocky man. I'm not sure if he actually believed that he was God's gift to women or if he laid it on thick for my sake, but it really rubbed me the wrong way. I was still very young and felt as if my whole life was ahead of me, so like hell I was going to let this guy push me around. I started to actually like him, but he seemed to like himself enough as it was, so there was no way I would add to that.

One night, we stopped at his place before dinner to have a drink and he said, "I'm going to send out an email real fast, here. You can watch TV and I'll just send it out." I was slightly insulted that he thought this dumb email needed to be sent out when I had given up one of my rare free nights I could have been out with my girlfriends or resting, but, hey, it was only a few minutes, right? I ran across a movie on the channel guide that I loved as a kid and asked while he was knee-deep into his email, "Oh my God! Hey! Have you ever seen this movie?"

Suddenly, H snapped at me, frustration seeping through his vocal cords. "I thought I told you to give me like five minutes." He went back to his email. I very calmly set the remote down, walked out of the room and right out the front door. Like an idiot, I had actually let him pick me up this time, so I didn't have my car. I went downstairs, hopped into a cab, and headed back to my apartment. I wasn't going to sit around and be snapped at by some dude just because he was buying me dinner. He called later and was flabbergasted that I would actually leave and walk out over that. I didn't find it odd at all. I didn't need to be there. I certainly had other things to do, and I didn't know him well enough for him to be snapping at me over things I had zero to do with. We made up eventually.

Time marched on. I had been dating H for a few months, but I never let him come over to my place. He had picked me up and dropped me off a few times, but I always had him drop me off two apartment buildings down, and I would walk in the front door and wave bye. When he would drive off, I'd walk outside over to my real building and go up to my apartment. Sure, you can say I was a being a little bit crazy, but one can really never be too safe. After some bad experiences with crazy men in the past, I'd learned my lesson.

One evening, I "stumbled" across his driver's license when he had to run downstairs for some reason. (When you are newly dating a man and he leaves you alone in his apartment, you go through his shit. Sorry, it's just an unwritten rule. You can find out a lot about a person from his things.) He had told me several times that he was 33 years old, which seemed like a bit of an age gap since I had recently turned 22. But we had a lot in common, and I figured it wasn't the end of the world.

Turns out H wasn't 33 at all; he was 36. What in the world would make him lie about being three years older, I had no clue. I called him out on it when he got back, and he assured me that he was just joking about being 33 and said that he thought I knew. 33 was his "Hollywood age." It was an inside joke with him and his friends, and of course I knew that information. Clearly, I didn't know that, and I also didn't like that he was playing this off as a joke when I had caught him lying. If you are going to be a liar, at least be a good one. (Although I would find out later that he was a much better liar than I had given him credit for.)

We worked through this problem, too. There were so many good qualities about him that every time he did something stupid, we would eventually make up. I would call him out on it, we'd have knock-down, drag-out fights, and he'd finally admit that he was being an idiot. He was so damn easy to forgive, with those soft, gentle eyes, smooth way of talking, and contagious charisma. He always said the right thing, even though I knew his actions didn't always match; I wasn't anybody's fool.

He also had a tendency to play petty kid games, which required special tactics on my part. If he walked into a bar where my friends and I were having a drink and tried to pretend he was a big shot, I'd walk past him as if I didn't even know who he was. If he flirted with a waitress a little too much, I'd bump into the guy eyeing me at the bar on the way back from the restroom and have a conversation. I was not about to let this man fuck with me. He figured it out eventually and stopped playing games.

Around this time, I had moved into a studio apartment off Sunset in West Hollywood. I loved my independence and started going out to Chateau Marmont alone for drinks at night, taking myself to the occasional movie, and stopping by coffee shops solo on my day off. I still saw H, but I also had great girlfriends. We explored LA, went to brunches, did yoga at Runyon Canyon, and hiked together.

Eventually, I started spending more and more time with H. He was fun, hilarious, and very easy to be around; even my friends enjoyed him and would invite him to come out with us. We had been "dating" over a year by this time and finally had the conversation about moving in together. At first, I said no, since the lease on my place wasn't up for another three months. But after many conversations with him asking me to move in with him and me saying it wasn't a good idea, I finally said I'd try it out.

Right after I met H, he had apparently run into some financial trouble. He'd had a very successful business for years before this and had been living the high life. He owned several cars that were so luxurious, I never dreamed I'd see one, let alone ride in one on a regular basis. Some kind of funding with his most recent business had a shift with the venture capital firm funding it, and he was in a bad spot. I had no idea how bad, but I could tell he was extremely stressed out.

I offered for him to move in with me until my lease was up. This would give him time and space to figure things out without having a ton of huge bills over his head. Initially, he thought this was a really dumb idea, but he did have to move out of his place, and I guess he eventually decided he'd survive. So, H and his multiple luxury vehicles moved into my studio apartment where his clothes hung on a collapsible rack; as for his cars, I only had one parking spot that wasn't permit parking, and that parking spot belonged to me.

Finding parking in LA, especially the neighborhood I lived in, was extremely difficult. There are basically 15 signs that say you can park there, but only with a permit after 8 AM every day, except on Tuesdays after 6, Thursday mornings from 8 AM to 12 PM, and Monday through Friday before 3 PM. Long story short, H spent most of those three months playing car shuffle, looking for spots on side streets, and moving cars to avoid getting towed. I don't know why he didn't just sell them to fix his financial troubles, but he wasn't a practical person. Eventually, he found a part-time job with a company through a friend doing some sort of debt settlement something. He started making pretty great money again and planned to stay there until things worked out with his company.

I had decided at this point in my career to go off on my own and start my own hair business that I would be in control of. I had started feeling stifled in my hair career early on. The higher-ups in my first salon seemed to always preach that "you have to pay your dues," or "after you put in the work for a long time you will get those benefits, too," and even "well, that's just the way it goes in this industry so get used to it." But I had never been one to shy away from hard work, and I had ideas for how I would make my own business better; it was always really easy for me to see what would improve the situation. I really enjoyed color and extensions, and if I focused on doing that, I could make more money in less time. And as I improved in that skill area, the good results would attract more clients. I was often told that I would need to take men's cuts and haircuts anyway, and I quickly realized this niche wouldn't allow me to live my dream until I went out on my own. H encouraged me to go off on my own and told me that if things went south, he would be there to back me up and help me get back on my feet. I would have never made the jump if he hadn't encouraged me and supported me to step out on my own.

At the time, I truly didn't think I could do something on my own or without help. All my friends had help from their parents, and I had really struggled thus far on my own. I don't mean struggled as in people let me starve, but I definitely have always been super hard on myself and wasn't where I wanted to be in life. It's almost as if I knew this other world existed, but I just couldn't quite find the portal to get to it. I was terrified to jump from working at a job to working for myself. The idea of going from employee to owner absolutely scared me. I believed that making money meant being hard on yourself and working nonstop, but at the same time, I held on to the belief that there had to be another way. I just didn't know what that way was yet.

With H's emotional and cheerleading support, I went out on my own. People were pissed. My salon owners lost their minds and took it personally, not understanding that I was answering a larger calling to my soul. It was hard and uncomfortable at first. People questioned my ability to own and run my own business, because of my age, or this or that. And I even questioned myself. In the end, it turned out to be one of the best learning opportunities I have ever had. Later on, some of the people who had questioned me or turned their backs on me when I went out on my own, messaged me and asked for advice. I was happy to give it to them, but it goes to show that it sucks being first sometimes.

My business grew, and H was starting to get back on his feet, too. He was clearly spoiled and used to living a certain lifestyle that didn't include a studio apartment with no dishwasher and no air conditioning. My lease was coming to an end, so we started apartment hunting for our first official place together. H wanted to spend an exorbitant amount, and I kept reeling it back in. I didn't care how much money I was making or how much money he was bringing in, throwing it away on rent just seemed stupid. We finally settled on a place that was outside my comfort zone in budget and way below what he wanted to spend. I guess you call that compromise.

We moved to the 20th floor of a high rise on the west side of LA, in a community next to Brentwood. We went from sharing a single room to having a two bedroom with an ocean view, and life was going well. My business was growing like wildfire, and I found myself busier and busier. Things seemed to be going well for H also, since he was always doing deals, with meetings here and meetings there (even though he somehow managed to sleep in until 10 AM every day and go to the gym for three hours to play basketball).

He started wanting to travel, which I kept turning down, because I needed to be in town for my business to thrive and survive. I had things to keep an eye on, clients to be there for, money to be made and accounted for. I also wanted to work fewer hours to have time to pursue other avenues. I wanted to learn about comedy, to write a book, to build a location independent business of some sort—but maintain a growing physical business made that difficult. I started to resent everything.

After a few really hard months dealing with the death of my grandmother, H sat me down and encouraged me to sell out of the hair business. He didn't like me working so much. I was rarely home, and, if I was, I was exhausted. I could be set financially for a bit, take some time off, and decide what else there was in the world that I wanted. I knew I wanted a business I could do from anywhere and which involved a lot less drama than working with a bunch of female hairdressers (it got to be a *lot* of drama). There just had to be more in life. He also said he'd help with the bills, so I could relax for a bit if needed. We could travel. I could have freedom. After a lot of debating, I decided to go for it.

I was completely terrified. Working hard was a purpose that had always defined me. It had given me meaning, definition, a rope to hold onto. In many ways, I thought what I did was part of my identity, even though I struggled with that. I never wanted to just be, do, or accomplish one thing. I was passionate about a lot of stuff. I enjoyed comedy, I wanted to make videos, I wanted to write, I wanted to have a company, I wanted to change the world. I had dreams and ideas that went beyond expansion. H made me feel as if anything was possible. He seemed to believe in me and would build me up, always boosting my self-esteem. It was addicting. He was the type of person that really thought big and had this larger-than-life personality. Everywhere we went, people knew him and liked him.

He made people feel special in his presence, and he carried himself with an air of importance. While he had a natural gift for charisma, I later realized it was a strategy that he had thought out and practiced over time. He actually told me that he had studied successful people and had learned that, if you didn't carry yourself in a fashion that showed an air of importance, some people wouldn't give you the time of day. I now realize he was talking about the wrong type of people. He also dressed for the occasion (although I did have to work on his fashion sense in the beginning and talk him out of the old school suit pant cut). As an entrepreneur who relies basically on connections, I now appreciate the importance of perception. It was a well-thought-out strategy behind his perception.

As a black man, H had grown up most of his life seeing the stereotypes and had fought really hard in many ways to overcome them. Maybe that's one reason why perception was such a strategic thing for him, and he was good at it. He carried that air of importance around so well that when we went on vacation, people would ask how they knew him, asking if he was a pro athlete or some celebrity. He loved it. He ate that shit up like it was morning oatmeal after a long fast. He'd always wink and say something cheeky like, "Yeah, something like that." When they'd press him about it, he would shift focus on them, responding with something like, "Ah, I'd rather hear about you. What do you do?"

At first, not working was hard for me, but I started going to the gym, learning more about nutrition (something I'd always been interested in), and catching up on all the shows I had missed for the past several years. I started taking comedic acting classes to explore that part of my passion. I read every entrepreneurial book I could get my hands on. Even though I didn't have to do anything for the first time in my entire life, I knew there was more that I could learn. I remember reading *The 4 Hour Workweek* by Tim Ferris and realizing there was a way to work less and ultimately make more. It was the first time I learned about the art of outsourcing and the genius behind leveraging your time. Then, I fell in love with the message behind *The Monk Who Sold His Ferrari*. I was slowly realizing that there were other ways to live beyond working constantly in back-breaking or spirit-breaking environments, that there was more to life, and that it required balance and being present in the moment.

My mom had always instilled in me the sense that life was about the little moments and that money wasn't everything. She raised us by example; even when we had nothing, she found ways to infuse joy into small things. We used to go to the Denver airport and ride the tram and escalators, in the days with looser airport security. All it cost her was a tank of gas and a trip to the food court, but she made it as fun as a trip Disneyland. From her, I learned to focus on the things around me that brought me great joy, and I found myself practicing that more and more. I also had the opportunity to travel more, fulfilling one of my passions. It was on one fate-filled trip to the Bahamas that my life changed in ways that I couldn't have imagined.

I had always been easy going about marriage with H and had never pressured him. I was still pretty young, and I wasn't sure if he was necessarily 100 percent "The One." Life was changing at a rapid pace, and although it seemed to be heading in a good direction, who can ever really be sure? He had been married once before to his high school sweetheart, and it hadn't worked out between them. H told me that, towards the end of their marriage, he had started to make amazing money for the first time in his life. He owned a mortgage company, and they had purchased several houses. Women started to notice him more, which led to more fights. He admitted to being unfaithful, because he hadn't wanted to settle down, and most women couldn't keep his interest for a long period of time.

Internally, I knew that it was all bullshit, that he had little self-control, and there was no excuse for that. I hoped it was a phase and yet never felt confident it was. I was honest about what I wanted, and I could only hope that he was doing the same. I would not allow infidelity in my life, which I told him up front, and if he wanted to be with a lot of people to make him feel special, then I made it clear that I wasn't capable of living that way. I guess I kept life interesting enough with my multiple personalities and penchant for dreaming big, since he stuck around. But he wasn't sure that he wanted to be married again.

When H made plans for us to go to the Bahamas, I wasn't surprised; he liked to go to a different country every New Year's. Our first year together, we went on a cruise to Mexico, which was my first time out of the country besides going to Paris to do hair for Fashion Week. He had been talking about taking a trip, and as I wasn't really working at the time, I didn't have any reason to say no. We booked the flights and, with his timeshare, we were able to reserve a beachfront room for a reasonable price.

New Year's Eve rolled around, and we spent the day exploring Freeport. We ended up at the casino, which I knew was going to be a problem with his lack of self-control. H always talked about how good he was at craps but never seemed to grasp that, when it comes to gambling, all you can control is mitigating your risk when it goes south. Hours later, long after our time had gone from fun to played out, H was glued to the craps table like his life depended on it, and was senselessly throwing away money. Now, I understand it was his money, and he was welcome to do so, but there comes a point when it just gets into the stupidity zone. We were in the stupidity zone. I tried to politely tell him we should finish up and maybe go do something else. I was the one who would pay for it ultimately when it affected his ability to cover the household bills.

"Just a minute." He didn't look up. "I need to win back my money."

"Yeah, but that's what people always think and they just keep losing more. Listen, if you have enough extra to be throwing away our rent money, just give it to me and pretend that you gambled. Then, I'll give it back and tell you that you won, okay? Surprise! Now, let's go."

He still didn't look up. "No, not now. I'm almost done."

Anger boiled my blood. "Whatever then, I'm not watching this. If you want to be an idiot, you can do it by yourself."

I walked away and found a slot machine in the corner. I figured I'd play out my voucher, get a cab back to the hotel, or maybe walk around downtown a bit. I wasn't sure why he was making things so difficult. He stormed by me on his way to the men's restroom, and I could practically see the steam coming from his ears. He gave me a side look on his way, and I could tell he was pissed off that I demanded he stop his game. I wasn't a quiet woman and never had been. He came out of the restroom just as I was wasting away the last of my slot spins. I braced myself for the impact of his bad mood as he walked up to me (attitude wise - he wasn't a violent person), but he could act like a child.

"Let's go get some dinner. Are you hungry?"

Phew, I thought. Crisis averted. He looked raging mad as he went into that bathroom and came out like Mary's little lamb, so I nodded and we headed to dinner on the pier. He was like that sometimes, with these extreme highs and lows. I didn't like it. After dinner, we sat enjoying some wine and watching the waves, listening to all the people partying around us in the busy downtown area.

"Hey, want to go back to the hotel and sit on the beach for when midnight hits?" he asked. He was always so show-boaty, so this seemed different. And more up my alley. We didn't have a ton of time, so we hopped in a taxi (actually, just a long, skinny van with no seatbelts), grabbed a blanket and champagne from our room, and went out to the beach. Besides a few people walking around here and there, we pretty much had the place to ourselves. As midnight struck, we touched glasses. "Cheers!"

H had always loved making toasts, so it was no surprise when he said, "I'd like to make a toast…" I just nodded. "Alright then…" He started off with how our relationship had changed him, how lucky he was to have me, and then he started to get down on one knee. It all happened so fast that I comprehended the gist of what he was saying, but I could never recite it to another person word for word. I'll just say that it was from the heart, it was simple, and as the fireworks started, he was there on one knee, holding a ring up, waiting for my answer.

I heard myself say, "Yes!!!" before I even realized I was speaking. In total shock and disbelief, I teared up a little, and he grabbed me and hugged me, screaming to passersby about how, "She said yes! We're getting married! Woohoo!" We played hip hop music, danced along the beach, took hysterical pictures of the two of us, and just celebrated in our very own style with no cares in the world. We entered the new year as an engaged couple.

The next morning, I woke up with a start. H was still asleep, and suddenly the events of the night hit me. I looked down at my finger to see a ring there and had to remind myself that those events did, in fact, take place. My stepmom had given me *The Hunger Games* books for Christmas that year, and I went out to our oceanfront balcony to sit in the warm air, watching the ocean and reading my book. I took a few minutes to stare at my ring, and, I'm sorry to admit this, but one of my first thoughts was, "Does this mean I have to change my Facebook profile status to engaged?" Something about that seemed so permanent. Marriage was permanent. Fuck. I was headed toward marriage. The ring wasn't my favorite. But what it symbolized made sense to me, and for that reason I found it to be special. He never asked if I loved it, so I never brought it up. Ultimately, he knew, though.

I had to take a few deep breaths and relax. Sure, I had thought as a little girl—even now as a girl who was still somewhat little—about the possibility of getting married, who the man would be, what my life would be like, things like that. Yet I had never planned a marriage in my head or thought about what kind of dress I would wear. I had never even been involved enough in anyone else's wedding to know much about them. I was more focused on my career, how that career would bring me money, and that money would bring me freedom.

As a child, I wanted a red convertible when I grew up. After telling me they hoped I would "marry rich to afford that kind of car," my family would ask if I wanted kids and where a child would sit. I told them that my kid could sit in the car with me. And when they asked where my husband would sit, because "most convertibles only have two seats, you know." I said, "Well, if I have a husband, he can just walk everywhere, I guess."

Those early conversations not only defined my feelings about marriage, they also set the state in my mind to have all that I wanted in the world. I didn't like how people assumed someone else would have to provide it for me, as if I wasn't capable or worthy of creating those things on my own. Perhaps I was hesitant about marriage because I had been told to marry rich, or that I had "champagne taste on a beer budget" repeatedly by people around me. Because they couldn't envision a certain kind of life for themselves, they couldn't envision it for me either, and I believed them. So, to be engaged was a big step for me. I tried not to fall too far down the hole of panic, and drank my coffee on the porch as I finished up my book, soaking in the solace the quiet morning brought. I did, in fact, end up changing my relationship status to engaged on Facebook. Engagement seemed to be ready for me before I was ready for it.

The next year flew by in the blink of an eye, and business for both of us took a turn. When H originally suggested that I stop working and sell out of my businesses, I believed that he wanted to have more time with me at home and more freedom to travel the world together. Later on, I realized that his motivation might be that he wanted me to help build businesses for him. He always complimented me on my intelligence and wanted to know my thoughts on business decisions and endeavors, even though he didn't always hear me. Like, actually *hear* me. After we got engaged, though, H started putting me down for not having a job, which was strange, because he had always lifted me up and encouraged me. After a few weeks of making comments about not working, he suggested I start helping him with tasks for his company. Being naïve, I figured, what else am I really doing with all my time? So, instead of focusing on the next big dream for Danielle, I was now focused on the next big business dream for H.

He had several businesses and was private about the main inner workings about his companies, but I figured that was just his need to be in control and to be "the man." I helped with many aspects of those businesses—always from an "outside" position—like building websites, finding ways to attract new business, client onboarding processes, hiring and training processes, employee manuals, how to streamline processes, backend systems, new strategies, growth and expansion opportunities, you name it. I did all the research and read books, and as a business owner myself, I seemed to have a natural intuition for these things. H sometimes struggled with this and saw it as a threat, as if I was saying that I knew better than he did. Yet, he didn't want me to own my own business, maybe because he felt like we would be competing and he didn't want to lose.

His businesses were a mess, judging from the parts I was allowed to see. Later, I would learn how messy things really were behind the scenes, how shitty he was at paperwork, and his screwy ways of keeping tabs on things. But what I could see at the time started to concern me, and I brought it up with him. He liked to seek out investors, which I thought was a stupid idea, especially when they were handled poorly. If your business isn't scalable on its own, then investment money is nothing but a life preserver with a puncture in it. Also, why would you want to start out owing people money if you didn't have to?

Our disagreements about business weren't enough to break us just yet, but the tension only got worse when we started talking about adopting a puppy. I had grown up with animals my whole life and had always been sad that I didn't have the time, the room, or the space to fairly take care of an animal, even though I desperately longed for one. I wasn't sure, at this stage in my life, if I was capable of putting something else above my own needs, but something inside me just said I really needed a dog. I brought it up to H a few times, as I thought it was only the right thing to do, since we shared the same household and all. But I didn't ask him to get his permission; I did it as part of going through the motions. I was getting a damn dog, like it or not.

H worked pretty often then, and when he wasn't working, he was at the gym or playing in a basketball game as part of a competitive adult league. I knew he wouldn't be taking care of the dog much, and I was fine with that, but for the first time in my life I had a bit of extra time.

"I have been thinking about it, and I'd really like to get a dog," I said one night over dinner.

"Why don't we just have kids instead?" H grinned. He had been dying to be a dad long before meeting me. Honestly, now, I think if he could have chosen between having a baby and having me, he would have chosen the baby, hands-down. All he ever wanted was to be a father.

"Yeah, so I really want a dog. I've been looking around quite a bit, and I'm not sure what I'd like. Obviously, I want to get something that is good for apartments, since we live in one."

"It's a condo," he muttered, correcting me.

"Condo, apartment, whatever." I rolled my eyes.

"No, it is important. We do not live in an apartment. It's a condo. And who is going to take the dog down the elevator 20 floors every time it has to go to the bathroom?"

"I will." I got up and put my plate in the sink before really giving him a piece of my mind. "But if walking a dog seems too difficult for you, you sure as hell don't need to be having kids."

We argued about it a lot in the coming days. I finally had to put my foot down. I didn't demand anything. I didn't throw a fit. I didn't ask for much. But it was my life, too, and I was getting a damn dog, even if it meant that I had to live alone in order to do it. I wasn't afraid to put my foot down, although I don't think I was stepping fully into my power at the time.

"Okay," he relented. But he wasn't sold on it.

After a few weeks of Internet stalking puppy sites, I had narrowed it down to a pug, since that breed would do well in our apartment (excuse me, our "condo") and could easily ride in the car. Plus, I had always loved their flat-nose look. I had fallen in love with a girl pug that a couple had adopted and couldn't keep for whatever reason (which is common in LA, since it can get so expensive). I convinced H this was the dog, and by the time he relented and said, "Fine, let's go look at it," I called and the dog was gone. I was happy she found a home, but I was truly heartbroken that it wasn't with me.

I finally came across a litter of pugs living with a family on the edge of a very sketchy neighborhood, so I waited until H could go that day with me. "We are just going to go look," I said. Ha. As a side note, I had gotten flak from a lot of people who said "adopt!" or "rescuing is the only way to go or you are going to hell." I get what they were saying, but I wanted a puppy to potty train and raise. Besides, if nobody buys the puppies that people have for sale, what happens to those dogs? Would someone answer me that? So, I'm still giving a dog a freaking home.

Anyway, when we pulled up to a house filled with some kids watching TV in the living room, the mom was at work, but they pointed us to the backyard to check out the puppies. They had the kitchen gated off and the back door open for the pups. The moment I entered the kitchen, I saw a little tiny baby pug sniffing around for food. I picked him up, and he curled up in my arms and looked at me with little baby eyes. I just knew there was no way he was being set back down. These people would have to pry him out of my cold, dead arms.

The oldest girl tried to show me a few other, bigger pugs they had. "That one, he's the runt. We call him Robin. This one's Batman. Are you sure you don't want Batman?"

"Yes, I'm sure. We want this one" I said. I nudged H, "Pay the woman."

As we drove home in the car, the puppy slept in my arms the whole way. "What should we name it?" H didn't even want the damn dog, now he wanted to name it?

"I'm not sure." I petted the dog's wet little nose.

"What about Morocco?" H suggested.

"Frankie. I like Frankie," I stated. And so, Frankie it was.

I potty trained Frankie, walked him, got up in the middle of the night the first week when he was whining, to check on him. I cleaned up his messes, I took him to the vet for his shots, took him to get neutered, bought books on his breed, and even tried several different kinds of food until I found the best one for him. When he was old enough, I took him to the dog parks nearby so he could socialize with different dogs from a young age.

I raised the dog by myself. I figured eventually H would come to terms with things and accept that we had a dog, but he never really did. He'd walk him once in a great while if he really had to and the whole time he'd just repeat, "Frankie, potty! Frankie, potty!" as if that somehow works (because it was such an inconvenience to walk him for five minutes). Frankie was my dog. That was the first time I really felt a gaping distance between us. For me, it felt that he didn't value what I felt was important in life. Even if he didn't like certain things that I liked, if they were important to me, there should be effort, compromise, and presence. Holes were starting to appear in the satin fabric of our relationship.

Chapter 4:
My Own Little Fairytale

We were engaged for over three years, mostly because I wasn't sure I was ready to get married. I had my doubts about marrying H, and the fact that he wasn't pressing the issue told me that he probably wasn't ready to get married either. He constantly pressured me to have a baby, but something inside me told me that it just wasn't a good idea. Not now, not then, not ever (at least with him). It just never quite felt like a good idea. But he was someone I could rely on and had a way of just taking care of things, so I thought we might have a shot at a happy life together.

One time, on a girls' trip to Vegas, my friends and I all checked our purses in together at the coat check of a pool party. Our purses had everything in them—money, IDs, cell phones, you name it—so when our Tanya with the wristband ran off to hang out with some guy and lost our only means of getting our belongings back, we found ourselves walking back to the hotel in bikinis. The front desk receptionist stopped us before we made it to the door and told us we couldn't enter the lobby like that. I told him I didn't want to enter the lobby like that either, but my friend had lost our things including the key to our hotel. Once he let us into our room, I called the hotel where we left our things, I called managers, I called everyone I could think of. Everyone told us that we would have to wait for our things to be turned over to the lost and found, which would take a day or so. We were in Vegas with no IDs and no money. We were shit out of luck.

I called H, and within two hours, we all had our things back. He just did stuff like that. We didn't wait at clubs, at restaurants, or in lines for much of anything, because he handled it somehow. And after being engaged for a few years with no wedding plans on the horizon, he decided to start handling that, too. He brought up that we should probably get started with the wedding planning process. But then he started to act weird, saying that he didn't want me to make a wedding website, which really pissed me off. He said, "I don't want to be on blast like that," basically saying that he didn't want our wedding all out there for the public to see, even though he posted everything he was doing all the time, bragging on social media. Sometimes he would even screen shot pictures of things and post them, claiming he was at an event that he never attended. I didn't understand his need to be seen as so cool, but I got over it. You have to pick your battles.

After we started planning our wedding, I got wind of some legal issues. He told me that they were civil and from his old company almost ten years prior. I looked over some of the paperwork, and he said he had to go back to court for it. He went to a court date for it in California, came home, and told me that there would be some back and forth, but that it would be fine. From what I could tell it was for some sort of mortgage deal he did a few years back and actually was civil. Yet it seemed there was more brewing. I could feel it in my bones.

Even though I wasn't 100 percent sure about going through with the wedding, it seemed like the logical next step. I was afraid of commitment, but I also knew that he was a good man who supported me and lifted me up. He wasn't perfect, but my family loved him, my friends loved him, and he was fun. We had been through a lot together, and it did seem like it was time for us to make a serious commitment or to split ways. I couldn't picture my life without him at this point, and I knew a family was very important to him. I didn't want to start a family without being married and just felt like there was no rush. If we were engaged anyway, we may as well enjoy each other and a marriage first.

Our wedding day was pretty perfect, really. People always tell you to prepare for things going wrong, but I had a great wedding planner, everything was set up in advance, and I went in ready to enjoy the moment. The weather was sunny, which was lucky as we got married at a beachfront resort, and the ceremony was quick but meaningful. I had never seen H look at me the way he did when I was walking down the aisle. It was truly a beautiful moment, the kind people in movies say they will never forget. The reception was amazing, and we had a DJ play hip hop, pop, and lively stuff that everyone could dance to. We paid for an open bar, as I was not about to torture people through a wedding with one drink token and a sea of awkwardness. I remember at one point the bartender ran out of alcohol and told me, "We were not prepared for you guys."

It seemed we were starting our own little fairytale.

Chapter 5:
How to Help Someone Destroy Your Self-Worth

e started off in complete marital bliss. But after a few months, H started acting strangely, in a way that I now understand was abusive. Unfortunately, it wasn't until later that I recognized that he was extremely talented at brainwashing. He was, slowly getting inside of my head and destroying my self-worth. I hate being the victim, and I hate the word "abuse," but I need to call it like it is. I had always been ferociously independent and had a very hard time allowing people to help me, so we struggled with this in the beginning. Over time, his manipulation changed me, and I became more and more dependent on him. There were small hints of it, here and there. I know, when most people talk about abuse and manipulation, you think, "How could they not realize it? What an idiot!" However, when you are in the situation, it is the small shifts over months and years that take their toll, until you wake up one day and you are operating on an entirely different set of parameters. And it's not until you separate from this person that you realize the true destruction that it was causing you.

H had an ingenious way of building me up, making me feel like the most gorgeous person in the world, and then, over time, knocking me down. He started to seclude me from people in small, subtle ways, telling me that I should stay home more and more, and making me feel guilty for spending time with other people. Soon, I heavily relied on him for companionship, for advice, for decisions, for everything. He made it blatantly clear that he wanted to be a family and to make decisions together, in a way that made me feel threatened rather than respected. I am a smart woman, but it crept up on me over time. Slowly.

He also required grandiosity in all things, and if it didn't meet his standards, then he would get angry. On one of our first vacations together, we were sitting in a Jacuzzi on a ship in the middle of the Pacific Ocean, looking out at this gorgeous scene. He wanted to smoke a cigar, because it looked better in the pictures, and when they wouldn't allow it, he got pissed. Everything had to be a certain way, with special favors and VIP privileges, or it wasn't good enough. This took a toll on our marriage from the beginning. I wanted to spend more time in the moment, savoring the small things, learning his scars and insignificant wrinkles. But he wanted me to be a Barbie doll to show off to his friends, the perfect wife who bought him presents and surprised him. This standard of living was difficult to keep up with.

He would regularly talk about how it was bad for men to go more than three days without having sex. (Being that he is in jail now, I find that to be hysterical, but that's a sunshine in my pocket thought for another day.) But if he was hoping that would make me submissive in the bedroom, he selected the wrong female. I always thought to myself, "Okay, so if after three days you don't have sex, you believe that you are truly unable to control yourself as a person? Then, you may as well go do whatever it is you would do after those three days now, and I don't want to be with someone with that little self-control." Even though I stood my ground here, it was clear that he made these comments to assert his dominance as a man.

He also underestimated my awareness when he was flirting with girls or doing shady financial things behind my back. I would get weird feelings or inklings that something was going on, and when I would ask him about it, he would make me feel like I was the most batshit crazy, insecure human being on the planet. He would swing from hurt, to kind in his response, to positively angry and offended, but, more often than not, his response was that I was crazy. Later, I found out that *every single time* I had that feeling, that inkling to snoop, that strange itch in the pit of my stomach, I was right. His deception doesn't enrage me as much as the fact that he made me mistrust myself and my intuition in the end.

He constantly and without reason made life-altering decisions without me, and I was over and over again left to deal with the consequences. Every time things got really bad, he would shower me with ridiculous gifts—take me out to fun places, whisk me away on a whirlwind trip, pamper me—until I forgot what we were fighting about in the first place. On top of that, he had a way of answering questions by talking in circles. You would think this would be an obvious red flag, but he was kind and heartfelt at the same time. He had a gentle and generous soul, or it seemed; now I find it all too convenient. I believe there is good in everyone, yet if you use what you are given for the wrong reasons, it can do an exorbitant amount of damage.

One night, about a year after we had gotten married, I woke up to a quiet and lonely house (kind of similar to how my heart and soul felt at the time). And I went to bathroom, got down on my knees, and prayed that God and the Universe would take from me that which no longer served me. I repeated it over and over. I knew that change would come. I let it go. Little did I know how that prayer would be answered.

Shortly after our one-year wedding anniversary, everything that had been simmering suddenly boiled over. H had been acting so strange lately that my suspicions grew. One day, while he was "working," I hacked into the live stream of his messages (he wasn't very smart and didn't realize that I knew all his passcodes and information, and could hack into his cell phone texts from his computer). Suddenly, popping up on the screen in real time, was my husband talking to another woman. I don't mean like "hey how was your day," but like "hey meet me at my place so we can bone," and "I wish I wasn't married," and "let's just have sex like we used to." Apparently, it was a girlfriend or fling of his from the past. I found another phone number I didn't recognize, that he had messaged about a hotel he was staying at a few weeks before. It showed up as a prostitute from San Diego. A quick Internet search revealed a Tinder online dating profile with his name and picture.

I was clearly married to a person that I didn't even know, on a cellular level, on an emotional level. And health-wise, after sleeping with all of those women? How disgusting. How dare he. I can't even describe to you the feeling that went through my body at that moment. After all the lying, the gambling, the legal issues, the messes he got into, the drama that he caused me. I had done nothing but support this man, believe in him, and uplift him. I stood by his side when the universe itself was conspiring to take him down, and how does he repay me? He knew from our very first date that my one and only serious line in the sand was infidelity of any kind. If you wouldn't do it in front of my face, you probably shouldn't be doing it. That is the respect that I think we deserve in relationships.

My body had an energy running through it that I had never felt before. The tips of my fingers prickled as if there was no longer blood running through my veins, but lightning. I wanted to pass out into a deep sleep and run as fast as possible all at the same time. I almost puked. I had to reread the messages. Yes, H could be a complete fuck-up. He could be a flirt. He could be an irresponsible, selfish, no-good asshole. But at the end of the day, I truly believed that he was loyal to me and would not do anything to disrespect me. I learned in that moment that I was very, very wrong.

I walked out of the office room and flipped over our bar cart in a fit of rage, breaking our collection of nice, crystal barware: wedding gifts of Baccarat glasses and Tiffany's wine stems. I didn't give a fuck. As the glass shattered in front of our door, I called him and told him what a miserable piece of shit I thought that he was and why. I grabbed what I could, picked up my dog, walked right through the pile of overpriced glass, and went down to my car. As I pulled out of the parking garage, H was pulling in. I expected him to be apologetic, to show some form of panic or remorse. I heard nothing from him. A few minutes later as I was already on the freeway, headed home to Wyoming, he texted me: "I cut my foot on the glasses you broke, you fucking bitch." I realized in that moment our love story was over.

I called a divorce attorney on the road. I had always promised myself that I wouldn't allow this type of shit in my life. Cheaters are cheaters are cheaters. Most of them have self-esteem issues that they are trying desperately to resolve, one vagina at a time. I didn't sign up for this type of situation, let alone the health consequences that could go along with them. I also took two very key items with me: H's laptop (for up-to-date messages and streaming spy services) and the one thing I knew he would actually miss, his prized Rolex watch. I took it as a bargaining chip, so that if he messed with any of my stuff or didn't allow me to come get it (a very real possibility given his need to feel in control), I had something I knew I could hold over his head to get my things back.

I drove straight through the night and arrived home in the wee hours of the morning. My dog got into my childhood bed with me. I slept briefly, woke up, and checked H's messages. It was the day before his birthday, and I had planned and paid for an entire trip to Catalina Island for his special day. I called to cancel the helicopter and the oceanfront room, but they refused to refund me at first. Then, the service representative asked, "But ma'am, why are you canceling with such short notice?" I couldn't believe I was saying the words. "I booked it for my husband's birthday, but unfortunately I just found out he's cheating on me, so I don't really feel like going on vacation with him." The manager refunded me right away. I was so thankful, but at the same time, I couldn't believe this was my reality. I didn't want the pity. I wanted my life back.

H finally started calling me and denying things at first, which really pissed me off. I had the messages in front of my face. Then, he finally said he was just saying stuff, that he was really sorry, and that he would do anything to make it right. I knew it was all bullshit, but I really didn't know what to do at that point. I knew I could never trust H again, but I didn't know where to go from here. I had helped build businesses for him. I had built my whole life around him. It didn't seem easy for me just to up and walk away, even though I knew that was inevitable. I wanted to be back in California. What would happen to our apartment? Where would I go? What would I do for work? He had convinced me to sell out of my hair practice and had pushed me to work with him from the get-go, because it gave him more control.

I talked to my brother-in-law while I was home. His marriage had ended after infidelity, and I asked him for his advice. I will never forget what he said to me. "Unfortunately, it's going to get a lot worse before it gets better. If this is what you know about, there is always more, and it's probably worse than you can imagine." I don't think I comprehended what that could mean at the time, but he was right.

That same day, I found out from spying on his messages that H had gotten two more girls' numbers, sent them flirty stuff, and even bought bottle service at a club for some girls on my American Express card. I called and cut off all my cards. I stopped answering his calls. The fucking balls on this man. His deception and disrespect clearly knew no bounds. H was out with one of our neighbors from across the hall, and from that day on when I would run into him, it would literally take everything in me not to scratch his stupid face off. I knew it wasn't his fault, but he knew we were married and he was totally fine with my husband flirting with chicks and trying to do God knows what, and then he wants to smile at me in the hall and ask me how my day is? My day fucking sucks because you just talked to me, thank you very much.

H finally flew out to Wyoming to talk to me about what had happened, and things got very confusing. He was extremely apologetic and wanted to work things out, yet he firmly believed that he could use the defense of "I never actually slept with anyone so it isn't cheating." I couldn't even handle it. All of it was cheating.

And if this was what I knew about, what I didn't know about was way worse. No doubt in my mind, he slept with multiple people while we were together. Not that it matters now. I just feel sorry for him. But at the time it was such misery for me.

After much conversation and confusion for me, the decision was made. He would drive back with me to California, and we would go to counseling. We weren't together, but we weren't broken up either. I knew I would never trust him again and that things were ending quickly, yet I took my vows seriously. I wanted to feel that, at the end of the day, I had explored all options, even though the only one I really wanted to explore was murder. I was curious what his explanation would be, and I kept going back to the thought of how he used to be. How we used to be. How we got here.

Why would he do this to me? What had I done to cause this? How was I not enough? Did I not make enough money? Was it because I wasn't slutty, posting naked photos of myself on social media? Was I not big/small/tall/short/tan/pale enough? How had this happened??? H was very (as he would call it) religious, and he constantly tried to force his religious views on me throughout our time together. He believed that you would be punished if you didn't do x, y, and z. If you weren't generous with your money all the time, his God would take it away from you. To him, his God "punishes." Yet, here he was, Mr. Holier Than Thou, breaking a sacred covenant. That was the most impressive part. I had my own beliefs (and they didn't include marrying someone just to screw other people).

On our drive home, I was so angry that I punched the steering wheel and broke my nail in half. For the first time in my life, I felt out of control of myself, my future, and my surroundings. Why was this happening to me? My mom had always told me, "If you don't know what to do, don't do anything," meaning that time will show you the best thing to do, and not to force the inevitable. So, I tried not to. I was riddled with anxiety, pain, depression, self-consciousness, and heartbreak. We went to marriage counseling, but it didn't go well. H couldn't tell the truth. He talked in circles. He didn't want to change. He offered no honest or helpful explanations. I thought these must be the worst and most awkward times of my life, but it was only the beginning.

It was weird and uncomfortable, not really being together but not officially saying "divorce" yet, either. Somewhere deep in my heart and soul, I knew I was done with this marriage. But I resisted and stayed in one place to avoid pain. I knew I could never forgive him for this. He suddenly was not the person I once knew. A short two weeks after all of this, I finally decided to go stay at my friend's place in Hollywood for a night, to have some fun and get all of these impending decisions off of my mind. As luck would have it, a lot of these decisions would be made for me when the rug was pulled out from under me, and used to almost beat me to death. The next day, I received the call that my "husband" was never coming home.

Chapter 6:

Nobody Envies Your Life. In Fact, Your Family and Friends Think Your Life Is Way More Messed Up than You Do.

May 22, 2015 (Day 2)

*B*less my mother. I swear she was made with an extra special dose of awesome. As soon as I called and told her that my husband was in jail, she said, "Okay. I am booking a flight right now. Can you pick me up tomorrow at 1:50? Thank. Friggin. God.

There would be nothing worse than handling all of this alone. Friends have reached out, invited me out, and offered to come over, but when it's been three hours since your life was destroyed, you kind of need a little time to process. And cry. And hyperventilate. And call a priest. And a psychic. And a stripper named Roxxy with two x's.

My day began as awful as possible. My eyes opened to the sound of my phone ringing, and I peered out to see the warm golden sun coming through our white silky curtains. The world was as it should be. I stretched and rolled over in my cozy bed to cuddle with....... My pug. Oh wait. No. It wasn't a nightmare.

I answered the phone to the Texas Department of Corrections. H was on the phone, making things up, telling me this was all a mistake that would blow over. He'd be out in no time, don't worry. Could I please get to the bank and withdraw some funds for myself as soon as possible? I asked questions, obviously. According to him it was really important that I go get the money out so I'd have some funds to live on. In hindsight, I'm sure it was him being selfish and trying to cover shit up, I'm sure, at my expense. I rolled into the bank looking like Britney Spears circa 2007, pre head shave.

Andrew, the kind and wonderful banker, explained to me after almost an hour of issues that the account had been frozen and there was strange activity on it and could they please talk to H as soon as possible please? I couldn't believe this was real life.

Then, my mom called to tell me her flight was booked into LAX instead of the airport right by my house. Not a problem, but I had to figure out how to ditch Andrew and his robot bank speech, because my five-minute drive just turned into an hour. I rushed home, fed my poor, neglected new cuddle buddy, and raced to the airport.

While I waited there for her to arrive, I tried my best not to have a mental friggin' breakdown. Waiting in silence with a bunch of strangers and thinking about WHY my mom was coming just made random sobs come. Not the sexy kind, more like "a donkey dying and people next to you moving away in fear that you are narcotics" type of sobs. Seeing several tourist women arrive into LAX wearing short shorts, high heels, and tube tops waiting to be discovered did help with some comic relief a little bit. Then I thought, "Give me six months, and I will probably be there myself." FML.

The minute she arrived, I felt human again for about three hours. She bought me an early dinner, some laughs, a margarita, and we came home and watched Netflix.

It was a funny show about these two divorced older women, and they were just getting back into the dating world. I swiftly realized that could be me. Probably not anytime soon, but eventually. Even if my husband and I did reconnect after his 14-year sentence, we would both be different people. We would have to start all over. As I mentioned before, I think, unfortunately, a devorche (that's divorce in fancy terms) was a must for protective purposes alone. Not to mention the recent infidelity issues.

That was when it hit me. I hadn't been on a date in over seven years. Did I even know how to do it anymore? Then, all I could think about were my dates with him, all the good times, because, hey, we could all use some extra torture. Last time I was on the dating scene, Internet dating was still for old people. Or, divorced people. Oh wait, that was me now. Or, soon to be. When was I supposed to take my ring off, anyway? My new sparkling wedding ring that he had surprised me with when things were normal. It didn't feel right yet, but I knew it would have to happen sooner or later. My spouse wasn't coming home until my eggs were 90 percent depleted. So, like, yeah. It had to happen.

Then there was this nagging feeling of "I should be doing something or making some sort of decision with my life, but I can't because I am overwhelmed and really there is nothing to do, and yet I feel I need to get started on them, but they would all be awful ideas I am sure." Seriously though, at 27, what did I want to be when I grew up? Where did I want to live? I thought I'd be knocked up by now putting a down payment on my dream home.

My mom already started in on how I should just move home for a while. 'Cause there is nothing like going from everything you have known in life for 10 years, to living with your parents in one of the coldest places in America that you left as soon as you could, to really remind you how well your life is turning out. Honestly though, bless her for it. It was nice knowing that I didn't have to be alone, that I had support and/or I wouldn't be a transient. So, some things were looking up.

It really was odd facing these kinds of decisions alone. Normally, I would just bring it to my spouse, and we would figure it out together. So, I tried calling him, but Texas Corrections doesn't take incoming calls. Commie whores. The realization that I would be making all major life decisions alone from here on out made me feel like my bum was in my throat. Except my bum wasn't my bum. It was the size of Nikki Minaj's.

Chapter 7:
Everybody Else Knows What's Best for You

Today was a better day. I sold my husband's diamond-encrusted midlife crisis Rolex watch to the jeweler we used to actually purchase jewelry from. The jeweler looked at me in a concerned way and said, "Will your spouse be mad that you are getting rid of this?"

"No, he knows I'm here," which was true.

But he did look at me with slightly concerned eyes, like, "Is this bitch selling his shit behind his back? Oh well, it's a nice watch." Then, he gave me a decent price for it, and I was grateful he didn't ask too many questions.

My mom loves jewelry and had a blast looking through all the pieces they had in the store. She fell in love with this really cool, unique ring and bought it for herself. Don't get me wrong, I am glad she spoiled herself, because she rarely does. At the same time, though, it was kind of depressing to sell your shit while someone was shopping for something sparkly. Such is life!

I texted a girlfriend about my thoughts the day before, on whether or not jumping back into the dating world would be the worst thing ever someday. The thought that I could be divorced and useless at dating before I even turned 30 was somewhat amusing but mostly awful. I couldn't think about anything but my present situation, so maybe I would just collect a gaggle of dogs and be the old/young pug lady. I also learned recently that a gaggle of pugs is called a "grumble." Sounds legit.

My girlfriend, who was currently with child, texted me back and said, "Not to worry! I will just raise my future baby son to your specifications."

Me: "What?"

Her: "You know, I will teach him to talk the way you want him to talk. I can raise him specifically for you so when you are ready to date again you have the perfect man! You can even pick his name."

Me: "I will not be a cougar Rumpelstiltskin."

Throughout the day, I had several message exchanges with different concerned friends.

Friend One: "Why don't you just move back to LA? I will find you a place, you can live nearby and even though it's for my own selfish reasons, it is exactly what you should do. Worry about work later."

Friend Two: "You can stay in our guest room, we can lease your apartment, we can figure it out! We need to get you working as much as possible and get you some more money coming in. It's best to stay busy."

My mom: "Come home for a few months. Or stay in the Lake Havasu house. Don't do anything for a while. Give yourself a break and mourn the loss of your relationship. You need to relax and move forward but don't decide anything too quickly. You need time to process things."

My sister: "Come home."

My dog: "Woof."

Basically, everyone had ideas on what I should be doing. Yet, I had no clue. How does that work? I had dinner with a friend and my mom this evening, which, can I just say, was delicious and wonderful; however, it kind of reminded me of the scene in *Pirates of the Caribbean* when the bad pirates try to eat and the food turns to ash, and they can't enjoy it because they are dead. The things you normally appreciate seem pretty useless when you're in a state of shock and disarray. But the food smelled good, and a martini never hurt anyone.

They both kept saying different things. One suggested removing my husband's things but hanging onto them in case something changed. Have hope! The other would then suggest moving on quickly. Sell all his stuff. Throw the rest out. Get what you can for it. He's fucked.

Then H's mother called and told me that I was supposed to put his clothes in his car, and, if he ever got paid some money back from some past things he was owed, that I was supposed to send her said money so she could fly here and retrieve his things and drive back. And because his father didn't have a car, I imagine he would start driving it every day and it would be basically shot by the time

H got out anyhow. The thing had more miles than Charlie Sheen already. So, it seemed my spouse had his own plan for what I was supposed to do as well. Not to mention, I would probably be expected to babysit said car and clothes until this phantom money showed up. Just another thing to deal with.

I was just a simple gal, living a simple life, one that involved collect jail calls, frozen accounts, my spouse's IRS audits, a bunch of items that belonged to a man who I happened to be in love with, who no longer lived here, and I was trying to get by with more bills than Hillary. I think I was currently the epitome of success. People of the world, take note!

Chapter 8:
You're Moving Down in the World (and Fast)

I showed my girlfriend a room for rent today. My room, in fact, with my California-king-sized-hand-carved-dark-wooden-beautiful-one-of-a-kind-bed. Above it hangs the white chandelier from Australia I bought one night on eBay after a little too much wine, only to find out that they didn't even make the right kind of light bulbs in America. Long story short, I was swiftly moving down in the world. It's okay. I would live in my guest room. Things could be worse. My lease wasn't up for months, and it would be dumb to try to pay rent on my own. But it was hard to rent out a home you'd worked for almost a decade to build, even if it was the best choice possible.

Let's get one thing straight—I am not bragging. I wasn't super rich with my husband. It's not as if I never worried about money. Yes, we had two incomes, but I wasn't ballin' out of control in fast cars and using a bidet and stuff. Sure, I rode in cars I never even imagined seeing as a child, but in this neck of the world, that's not obscene. Our life was good, though. We had fun, flexibility, some nice things we had acquired together. More than that, we had each other. I had someone that legitimately adored me (or at least that's how I perceived it at the time). He treated me well, opened doors for me. Hell, he even planned my bachelorette party with my gay best friend and paid for everyone to fly there and surprise me on

Valentine's Day. He didn't even go, as he didn't want to intrude on the "girl" fun. Probably because he had plans with another girl at the time, but I couldn't comprehend that then. I didn't know enough.

I don't want to make this about him, either bashing him or remembering him with overly rose-colored glasses. The man could be a badass at times. So yeah, giving away his things, or selling them, was hard. But, all of this is to say that I was not starting my life over with a fat bank account and a plan. I wish I had been more gold digger than that. I didn't have the time or information to realize the situation I was facing. Trust me, there were times when I could have left scot-free with a lot of money and never worried about another thing. So, reading his letters about how I was abandoning him because he's in a tough spot was hysterical to me. I was distancing myself, because he was not a truthful person. At the same time, watching people tour my bedroom, or selling his watch, all of these things that we had worked toward together, was extremely difficult. I felt like he was dead. Until he called.

The next day, I went to church with my mom. I usually don't love church (I find God more in nature, personally), but the one we went to with Pastor Rick Warren at Saddleback was pretty cool. I don't love their "give the church all your money if you have faith" vibe, but besides that, there was good stuff in the service. He talked about what to do in the trials of life, the waiting periods, how to have faith, how to set goals and believe in yourself, how things are rough for everyone, and how we can come out on top if we just act as if our prayers are already answered. I took my mom for some authentic Vietnamese pho after, and she got teary-eyed several times and told me that she hadn't been sleeping well. I guess I hadn't realized how much the awful things that I was going through affected my family. Sometimes, I felt as if the Universe was somehow conspiring against me, which I know sounds doubtful, but hear me out.

Our apartment building once caught fire (the whole 10th floor- we lived on the 20th), and of course my husband was out of town at the time. The alarms didn't go off but luckily I saw the billows of giant smoke floating in front of our window, so I had to run our pug down 20 flights of stairs inside my sweater. People ask you what you would take if your house was burning down. Well, now I know. My purse and my pug. That's it. I told H about it when he called right after and he thought I was being dramatic as I sat outside our home watching the building engulfed in flames, thinking we had lost everything, until he later saw it on the news. As I drove away, the movie theater two blocks over had the placard on the front entitled, "Burn, Baby Burn." I can't make this shit up. I don't say this to make you feel sorry for me but to show that life is never perfect, and when things go to shit, the best you can do is claw your way back up.

I've had unimaginably amazing times and have achieved things I never even dreamed were possible, but I've also been through many a tumultuous moment that tested my strength and determination. We all go through times like that, but nobody likes to post "wow my life sucks sometimes" on Facebook. And if you are that person, please stop. Everyone hates it.

Anyway, here I am, left with an extremely overpriced apartment I can't afford (and didn't want in the first place), selling shit that belongs to someone else, and I am on my own again. And my spouse wondered why I refused to move in with him after several years of dating. I had my own shit, and, even though it wasn't spectacular, it was mine. No one was taking it from me. Some good that resistance did. It makes me think of the naive and the ignorant, and I actually envy them. Thinking too much in times like these can make you your own worst enemy. I wish I could think, "oh, my spouse isn't here anymore, it's just adventure time!" #richkidsofbeverlyhills

Seriously though, not to harp on it, but I come home and turn on *Keeping Up with the Kardashians*, and I seriously wonder what the obsession with them is. I get it, I find them pseudo interesting myself, and yet they have no real problems. Yeah, Bruce wants to be a girl. He lives in a mansion in Malibu and can afford a sex change and got a TV show from announcing said sex change, which he was paid very handsomely for. It took courage, I am sure. But things could be worse. Kourtney is only ever mad at Scott, and doesn't seem to do much but stay home, bitch about him, and drop kids out of her womb. Kim just talks about her awesome friends and her awesome this and awesome that. Their problems never go deeper than the surface, and their good times and bad ones are reflected in this. Their children will never have to worry where to live or what to do for work if something bad happens.

I want this for myself. I want this for my kids. Sure, my husband wasn't Ray Jay or a professional athlete, but he was better looking than them, and we built several businesses together. Businesses that I now wanted nothing to do with. We owned part of a restaurant in Beverly Hills, a medical device company, and a marketing company, all of which I contributed to and helped build. But I was filing for a default divorce or annulment, and I was requesting none of it. I would literally only walk away with the debts he left me with, because I distrusted him so much, I wanted nothing to do with him, nothing in common, no ties, nada.

Seven years of blood, sweat, and tears, and our finances are leveled. Bye bye. And I didn't even care because I just wanted to be rid of him. So, don't even start with me about the Kardashians—no, I did not want to be like them. Yet, you can't help but admit that they have built a substantial empire based on being some version of themselves that most everyone in their family can rely on at some time. Now, why the fuck am I talking about the Kardashians? As I said, when you watch their weirdness and it looks more appealing than yours, you know you are moving down in the world (and fast). So, how did I pick myself back up?

Chapter 9:
You Aren't Doing Misery Correctly

A friend of mine texted me to ask me what I had planned for the future, now that I was more or less married to Charlie, the voice from *Charlie's Angels*. I told him I was working on doing some real estate with my friend Paula while I brainstormed what kind of business I actually wanted to build for myself. He asked me what I thought about going back to work doing hair. Listen, I am in no way demeaning the hair industry or the people that work in it—I did myself for almost six years— but I was like, uh, I owned a hair business before and worked for myself. I learned quickly, built my way to the top, and accomplished everything I could have ever hoped for. I even got to do hair for Paris Fashion week once, in friggin' Paris! How cool is that. Just because I'd lost everything, didn't mean I needed to backtrack to square one in EVERYTHING.

He said, "Why not? At least it's something solid to do." So, working a career short term that I knew I didn't want to follow through with in the long term was the best idea possible, because I couldn't do any better, right? I mean, maybe at some point, but I'd do it on my own terms instead of starting from square one. Believe me, I knew this person had my best interest at heart. I knew all of my friends and family did. It just seemed like they forgot that I had survived for a long time by myself before I met H. I did have a life before this, and I would have one again. I had my sights set on bigger things. What can I say, I'm a dreamer.

I talked to another friend tonight who couldn't get a hold of H and wanted to know if everything was okay. I finally told him what had happened, because he was a close friend and former business partner of his, and I thought I should inform him at least for clerical reasons. While we were talking on the phone, he told me that it was okay to break down and be upset and stuff. It seemed like I disappointed people if I was too upset, and I also disappointed people if I was not upset enough. So, everyone had their opinions. Friends asked me what I was going to do now. Should I stand by him? Wait it out? Was I riding off into the sunset with Val Kilmer like it was a 1980s movie, wind blowing in the hair? No. It doesn't work that way.

I said to myself, what can I do today to make life better, and what can I do to make sure tomorrow is better than today? That was about as far as my telescope reached, and even then, sometimes it was blurry. So, my decisions may seem rash and my logic may seem crazy, but nobody really explained to me when I was growing up how to survive your new husband suddenly being thrown in prison for over a decade. I didn't know how the process worked. I just knew I could only help myself right now, and that is what I was trying to do. Oh, and I needed to help my pug. Cause he needed help getting up onto my bed and stuff. Well, while it was my bed anyway. I rented out my master and the furniture to my best friend Ari, so I guess we all had to be flexible. Thank God for her.

When I went to work today, Paula kept looking at me as if she was searching my face for uncontrollable emotions or wounds, as if this nastiness would leave a scar like a Glasgow smile. After showing properties, we went to return phone calls from her home office. I was on the phone with a new client, and H called me

20 times. Obviously, I couldn't answer it, since it would take me about 10 minutes to navigate all the prison phone system menus and accept the charges. I knew it was the last time he could call me until tomorrow morning, and I had an attorney meeting tomorrow to file for divorce and protect myself from ramifications of Lord knows what else he had done behind my back.

Unfortunately, when I had informed him of my meeting with the divorce attorney earlier in the day, his response was not exuberant, and I could understand why. He told me how he had been nothing but faithful to me while he had been in there, and he hoped I could do the same. Umm, when you were out of jail you screwed around behind my back, but now you are behind bars with nothing but dudes, and so somehow that is considered being faithful? Everyone do a handclap for this. Impressive.

However, as I mentioned, there was no right way to do this. He even started asking me not to sell some of his stuff that he had already told me to sell, as he was hoping to get an appeal or some sort of shock probation thingy. Selling stuff seemed so permanent, and I didn't like it. But the longer I postponed coming to terms with the circumstances, the harder all of this would be on me, on him, on both of us. So, what was the right thing to do? Where was my fairy jail-mother?

I found out later on, though, that he actually plead guilty, so I kind of think if he goes before the court and says, "Just kidding! Wait… what do you mean no take takebacks? Can we do a tradesy?" that they will probably not respond very well.

At the end of the day, I think he was settling in and looking for a way out, and it's not that I didn't want him to find one. I wanted nothing more than for this to go away for him. I don't wish jail on anyone. But it was not my problem. He got himself there. But, hey, on the bright side, his rent was paid for, his meals were prepared for him, and he even had cable for goodness sakes. Prison is by no means a cake walk, but I did have to survive on the outside without him. My meals weren't served and my rent wasn't paid for. Hell, the cable company even expected a check, and that is some bullshit. I'm supposed to pay to watch other people pretend to live inside of a box? I cancelled that shit. Netflix all the way, my people.

Really though, I tried to explain to him that appeals *this* and motions *that* may not work, or, if they do work, they'll take time. I still had to survive in the meantime. Nothing was promised. So, I knew he would prefer me to wait, but he wasn't the one who was having to live life on the outside without their spouse anymore. With everything he had done, even if he did get out, he would not be welcome here anymore.

Part 2:
The Bottom

Chapter 10:
The Best Way to Get over Someone Is to Date Pretty Much Anyone Else

I had dreaded the day when I would have to start dating again, but a few weeks after my appointment with the divorce attorney, I found myself doing shots in a Vietnamese restaurant, courtesy of a dark and handsome stranger at the end of the bar. My friend, Paula, was having an excruciatingly hard day, so we went out for some pho and wine. Enter said stranger. He ordered a shot of Fireball that was basically the size of a bottle, and then he ordered shots for us, too. I refused to do Fireball, so we settled on wild cherry Stoli, because we are classy like that. I remember looking at Paula and saying point blank, "I'm going to be wasted after drinking this." And wasted I was.

He said his name was Jamie, and he was staying at his cousin's house around the corner. Next thing I know, the guy's cousin is in front of the restaurant, yelling at Jamie for drinking so much. #awkward. Then, the cousin sat down and started talking to us. To make a long story short, he basically asked if I would like to be his wife and kept staring at me intently. I was wearing my wedding ring at the time, and I'm not sure if he noticed, but he asked if I was single. I said I wasn't sure, but why not. We got into a discussion about it, and I said I was having my marriage annulled or otherwise ended, which is probably the best choice right now. Obviously, I was completely blindsided by this encounter and felt a little guilty. But why? I guess I was raised with some sort of integrity.

After moving on to the next bar, I asked what kind of music he liked, and he said, "gangster rap." With stars in my eyes, I could not believe that fate had led me here; gangster rap is also my favorite music, and I use that exact term. I decided at that point that he was okay in my book. I think it was around this time that I removed my wedding ring and put it in my back pocket.

Paula, who does not miss much, said, "You need to slow it down with this guy."

Me: "I'm not trying to date him, it's fine."

Paula: "Then why did you take your ring off?"

Me: Crickets. Shit balls.

He then says, "Do you even know my name?

"Yes," I slurred, "It's Jamie!"

He laughed and replied, "That is my cousin's name. I will text you mine." This shows how in the game I am. Well, we'll call him Tom. His name was definitely not Jamie. The next day, he called me and asked if I would like to hang out. I told him to come get me, and he came into my house for a few minutes. Let's just say that my house was completely trashed from my whirlwind of a week. I was operating at level zero of "trying to impress people." I'm talking tampon boxes all over the counter, clothes on the floor, my wedding photos on the wall, my ex's clothes on the floor.

Being the direct person Tom was, he asked whose clothes they were. I said my husband's. Then, he asked how long he was in jail for, and I said 14 years. Don't sell drugs. (Just kidding. But really, I said that). At this point, I realized after we got outside that if he was any sort of normal, he would have realized how fucked up my life was and deleted my phone number immediately. But he didn't. We stayed in touch, had long and exciting text conversations, and went out a few times here and there. So, if you were wondering how it is to date after being in a relationship and marriage for almost a decade, well, it's pretty awkward. Yet it's a whole lot easier when you really just don't care.

Somehow, it was helping me get my head on straight to move forward with my life and do the things I needed to do. I was smiling, laughing, and feeling special for the first time in forever. The past few years with my spouse had been extremely difficult for me, and I guess I had been tortured enough. So, I had decided to let myself have a little fun. I had gotten into too many serious relationships without ever really dating, you know, playing the field. Men do it all the time. I decided I was going to date. I was going to go on dates with pretty much anyone and everyone to see what exactly was out there in the world. And I made no apologies for that. And before you get all "Mom" status on me, don't worry; I took Ubers, went home alone, and used good judgment.

Chapter 11:
Just When You Think You Have Hit Rock Bottom, Grab a Shovel

*L*ately, I had been avoiding calls from my ex. I was sorry for everything that he was going through, but every time I talked to him, it forced me to face the jarring realization that I was in purgatory, not moving forward or backward, stuck in this middle limbo of life. He wanted me to stay stuck in the past. He would bring up all the good and happy times as if nothing had ever happened. Him being in jail was always "a mistake." Someone else's fault. Oh, and he never "actually" cheated on me, he was just talking to a bunch of girls about inappropriate things. Even if that were true (it wasn't), that was cheating to me. I didn't like the feeling, and it quite frankly pissed me off. But this time, I decided to answer, and he was in tears. He explained to me that he was now the guru of Jesus as he had fasted for the whole day (which, come on, was me pretty much every day), and that a lot of answers had been placed on his spirit. He told me that he needed to confess EVERYTHING to me. Then, he stated two things:

#1. "I haven't been the best man over the past 20 years, and I have hurt a lot of people. You don't deserve this. You are the most amazing woman I have ever known."

#2. "I did *try* to cheat on you and that was wrong of me. I am just now realizing it."

I mean, those were great and all, but he gave me no real tangible information that wasn't already blatantly clear to me at this point.

"Try to cheat on you."

"Not the best man."

Even in his "confession" he couldn't be 100 percent truthful.

I needed to get out of the house, so it was perfect when my neighbor D invited me out to LA for the night. The city was a 45-minute jaunt for me, and D was nice enough to give me a ride. In the elevator on our way out, for some reason he asked me not to tell our mutual friend Paula that he was driving me up there. So, when she asked what I was up to, I told her that I was driving myself and meeting up with him. I didn't see why this was such a big deal, but I just wanted to wear my new dress out, so with the stress of everything else going on, I didn't really care.

We went to Mr. Chow's, a high-end Chinese restaurant with Warhol artwork hanging on the walls, and met a couple of our other friends there, D's friend "Sam" and two of his girlfriends. We all started chatting and having some drinks, and one of the girls, who we'll call Blondie, was sitting in the corner. She kept giving me cunt face from across the table for some reason and didn't say much to me. Her friend, whom we'll call "Cassandra," was quite effervescent and spiritually cool. I really dug her vibe.

The food came, and as D offered me some fried rice that cost somewhere around $55 for a pot, I saw a bug the size of a cockroach crawling across the top. Apparently, it was a June bug, but as I am not an expert in these things, I just knew that it probably wasn't good. The bright side was that they sent us over a bottle of Veuve on the house, and the waiter poured us all a glass.

D said, "I just want to make a toast, to Danielle being newly single. Honestly, she has really been through some shit. So, here's to her." I thought that was very kind, and we all sipped on some liquid sunshine. Suddenly, Blondie in the corner over there leaned forward with her shoulders and pointed one long finger toward us. "I thought you two were a couple?"

"No," I explained, "He's my friend and neighbor. But we're not a couple."

"Oh, I thought you were together," Blondie said, yet again.

"No. Not a couple," I repeated.

"Oh." She sat back in her chair. Then she proceeded to chat with him across the table, "So D, what is it that you do?"

I laughed to myself, only because I totally saw that one coming, and I was surprised it took her until course number two to dial in on the poor guy. The gentleman next to me, Sam, made good conversation and we chatted a bit. We went to Chateau Marmont after that, and the whole rest of the night Blondie was giving me subliminal digs, probably not even on purpose, just trying to assert her dominance so that D would zero in on her or something. I had been in this situation dozens of times and I really didn't care, so I just brushed it off.

At one point, D sat next to me at our table and pulled his chew can out. So, I thought, "What the hell. I'm from Wyoming." He passed it to me, and I put a little bit in. This stuff, if you have never tried it, hits your system pretty much instantly. You go from normal to uncoordinated fast, even though you can still think clearly. Obviously, I was not a chewer or it wouldn't have had such a strong effect on me, but when in Chateau Marmont, right? Being the amateur I was, I had to excrete my chew spit, and what better place to do it than in my empty vodka soda. I bent the straw in half so it would be easy to recognize, and when I was satisfied with my chew buzz, I discarded it and put a cloth napkin over my chew glass so there would be no mistakes.

D decided to walk around the bar and check things out, so I obliged and went with him. We played a game where we pointed out people and said, "Your team," which I didn't really understand because it was his game with his other friend, but it was amusing nonetheless. We returned to the table and Blondie was holding a drink She took a large swig of it, and started gagging. "OH MY GOD! I THINK I JUST DRANK CHEW SPIT! WHO THE FUCK IS CHEWING!" She gagged. "Are you chewing?" Pointing at the man next to her. "Are you chewing?" Pointing to another guy. "D, are you chewing?" Everyone was shaking their heads no. She went through all the men at the table and repeated, "Who the fuck would do that? Who is chewing?!"

I responded, "Wow, yeah, how disgusting, who would do that?" D gave me side eye. Oh, sweet, sweet irony. How karmic. I felt bad, but who drinks from random glasses on a table? I brushed it off that at least it wasn't a roofie. So, I felt like she won tonight, you know, in a way. D drove us back to our building and deposited me at my door like a perfect gentleman. I had survived thus far. I went to bed with my little pug and dreamed of better days.

The next day, my good friend Josh, who I was doing some work with and really looked up to, invited me over. It was Father's Day, so Josh's in-laws came over, they fed me, and we had some laughs. His wife gave me some great advice on how to reset, wipe the slate clean, and said that I should look at the situation as what I have gained instead of what I have lost. It was wonderful. In another way, it was bitterly ironic, as I had been discussing and thinking if I wanted my own family only months before, and now I was single watching someone else's family celebrate. But it was nice to be around some positivity and laughter.

I drove home that night, and by the time I got home, Paula wasn't answering my texts anymore. I got a call from D, "What did you tell Paula about last night?" The only thing I could remember telling her was that we didn't drive together, as he requested. He replied, "Well, I kinda told her that we did drive together, and now she thinks you lied to her. I told her I told you to tell her that, but she's upset about it I guess." Great. Now, I have to deal with this drama, too? I put it to bed for the night, but I reached out to Paula the next day. She said she felt like my loyalty was with D and not her, and that she was upset and her feelings were hurt.

I felt like an asshole, but honestly, I wasn't even thinking about Paula or D. Paula was a grown woman, and where I went and with who was not her business. I had so much going on every day that I really didn't think it mattered how I got to LA or why anyone would really care, since I was a few years away from 30, single, had just lost my husband, and was completely alone in the world. Apparently, it was the wrong move. I get that. Honestly though, did I not have enough shit going on? Did we really need to do the drama thing? Oh well, not everything was about me in this world. I apologized and assured her that it would not happen again. I can admit when I screw up. Other people still have feelings. It's just a part of life.

I checked the mail, because I was hoping my divorce paperwork had been returned, and inside was a letter addressed to me from an attorney. My heart literally skipped a beat. "Here it comes," I thought. I didn't know what "it" was, but I did know it was most likely not positive, as mail from law firms never tends to be good. I got upstairs as quickly as possible, navigated the small talk that I didn't want to do on the elevator, and tore it open. Inside:

Dear Danielle, owner of The MDR LLC,

Your business loan is in default. The new total due is $11,270.00 including your past due amount of $1,270.00. We will attempt to collect, blah blah blah.

Loan information:

Lender: Kabbage something

Borrower: Danielle

Blah Blah.

Signed,

Mr. Attorney

There were a few problems with this. I did not, nor had I ever, owned The MDR LLC. I'd never applied for a loan from Kabbage (or anyone else for that matter), and I sure as shit did not owe anyone $11,270.00. I realized, with zero Sherlock Holmes skills needed, that my husband basically took my social security number, birthdate, and who knows what other information, to get a business loan after he had been denied. I called the attorney immediately and explained the situation. He told me that the money went into an account that was not in my name, and that they did see correspondence with my husband, so it shouldn't be hard to prove it wasn't me. Unfortunately, I had to fill out a police report for identity theft and do all this other stuff to clear up this situation. As if I didn't have enough shit on my plate.

I felt completely out of control in my life, and I didn't know what the future held anymore. I had literally been working nonstop. I felt like I was skydiving 99 percent of the time without a parachute, and I sometimes had panic attacks. I had lost a substantial amount of weight, my hair was falling out in handfuls (literally), and I had lost my husband and partner in life. I handle stress pretty well, but, apparently, my body does not.

However, nothing, nothing on this earth could have prepared me for the betrayal that I felt when I opened that envelope. After every lie he had told me, basically forgetting to tell me he would be going to prison, denying, covering up, not telling the whole truth, cheating on me, I stood by him the whole time. And this is how he repays me? Using my information to get just another 10 grand to blow on Lord knows what. And he had apparently done it right before he went to prison. 'Cause who cares at that point, right? Facing 14 years behind bars? May as well go out with a bang and screw over your spouse even more, while you're at it. Twist the knife.

I couldn't. It was the final straw. It broke me. I literally felt split in half. I went to my knees on the ground and tears spilled out of my eyes. "You are being such a pussy," I thought. But I couldn't get off the ground. The worst part was, I couldn't even pick up the phone and scream at him. I had to wait. And wait. And wait for him to call. The steam built up inside me slowly. I felt like a boiler on high, a pot bubbling over. When he called this time, which was about 24 hours later, I let him have it. I didn't even let him talk. I had zero patience at this point, and I told him I knew what he had done and how pathetic his "confession" was. He could have probably included in that poor excuse for "coming clean" that he defrauded me, the only person who had always had his back. I won't repeat exactly what I said here, but it was ruthless.

I feel slightly bad to this day about what I said to him, but it had to be done. After being fed shit sandwiches for seven years, that piece of paper was my turning point, and there was no going back now. I told him I was going to keep this very simple. "I am going to ask you this one time, and one time only. I already know you took out this loan. I already spoke to the attorney. I have it on paper in FRONT of me that you did it. I am sick of being lied to. All I have ever wanted is for you to be honest with me. So, I will give you a chance to be honest for ONCE. Did you take out this loan in my name? If you lie to me so help me God I will hang up this phone, I will change my number, and you will NEVER hear from me again. Do you understand? Did you take out a business loan in my name?"

He responded, "No."

I repeated, "Ok. I have the documents with your signature. In front of me. I already know that you did it. The attorney for the company even told me that you did it. It was deposited into an account in YOUR name. So, I will give you one last chance. Did you take out a business loan in my name?"

He paused, probably mulling it over. And responded, "No. I didn't."

So, I hung up the phone. And I changed my freaking number.

This was truly the turning point for me. I was finally ready to move forward, declare myself single, and build my own life. It became official. I decided to continue my dating ventures, keeping it casual and using it as a distraction, research if you will, into who I was truly looking for as the new Danielle.

#1. I want to relearn myself at this age.

#2. I'd like to know what is out there in the world.

#3. I need to invest everything in myself.

After working all day, I decided to go down with Paula to the pool and catch some sun. I was mentally and physically beat, so afterward, I went upstairs, showered, and fell asleep immediately. At 9 PM, my phone started blowing up and woke me out of my pseudo-coma. It was a man named Wes. He had asked me out a few times, and I didn't remember agreeing, but hey. He informed me that he was here for the date that I agreed to (when did I do that?), and was I coming downstairs now? I rolled out of bed, checked myself in the mirror, and I was literally wearing a pink bath-robe and my hair made me appear to be a victim of electric shock. I brushed it as best as I could, threw on a black dress and rolled downstairs like a hobo with access to a truck stop shower.

First of all, he opened the door for me like a perfect gentleman and took me for martini's, which who knew there were places open here until 1 am on a Sunday? This town was like Pleasantville, that never happens. We sat in these large picture windows in the bar area and took in the waves.

I asked a lot of questions about him, mainly because I think people like that, and it's a fun game I learned from my mom. You ask as many questions as you can about another person and just see if they ask you anything. He didn't really. I was not attracted to him, but he did seem very nice, and it was sometimes good just to be out and not thinking about my overall situation for 20 minutes. And it's fun to learn about other people, what makes them tick, how they got to where they are now, their strengths and weaknesses. These things were way easier for me to spot than seven years ago. He dropped me off back at the house and went in for the kiss, at which point I had a decision to make. Did I lead him on and try it? Or did I diss him by literally turning the other cheek? I went with the latter, casually turned to get out of the car, and thanked him for the nice time.

The next day, I woke up to approximately eight e-mails from my ex (via his surrogate life keeper, aka his mom). They went from bad to gibberish, informing me of what to do with all the money he didn't leave me, and reprimanding me for selling his Rolex for like six grand to buy a house (umm, what?). Like, off-the-rails type stuff. Not only that, but he was clearly trying to save face (from *prison*), because he copied my friends and family on the email, stating that I had plenty of money and that he didn't owe me anything, and would I please pay off the business loan that he took out—illegally, in my name—with all of the cash that grows on the tree outside my house. One of my girlfriends was pregnant and did not need to be harassed with 100 emails that had nothing to do with her. My friends and family had had enough of him, and I didn't understand what he and his mom were trying to do except drive me freaking insane.

I couldn't take it anymore. I called his mom from a private number. I had never been anything but nice to her, so I am sure she was taken aback when I said the F word repeatedly and told her that I would be happy to make this worse for both of them. I told her, and I quote, "I am DONE FUCKING with you people! Leave me alone! If you keep emailing my friends, harassing my family, and bothering me, I would be glad to take the entire file cabinet full of my spouse's documents and turn them over to the IRS, the DEA, and whoever else would like them. I'm sure there is nothing but pure gold in there. I don't give a fuck anymore. Do you hear me? Leave me the FUCK alone!"

I was dissolving our marriage, not seeking spousal support or requesting any of our assets. I was not bad-mouthing him all over town or trying to be insensitive or accusatory. I was not bitter or asking for the world on a silver platter. I literally just wanted the money that I was owed (which I will probably never see) and to be left in peace. Actually, I didn't even care about him paying me back at this point. Just peace would be nice. But the debt he left me with was so not cool. Did I mention he racked up my credit card as well to almost 20 grand before leaving? Yep, there's that, too. You know, the one in my name that he had authorized usage on. According to the stories I had seen and heard since he had been away a little over a month, maybe I even got off easy compared to most. After the call with his mom, she obviously emailed me and my mother a bunch of nonsense, claiming she may call the Wyoming authorities. Okay. And all my ex did was pay for things for me and my friends and family. Okay.

I was pretty sure he spent all of his money on himself, and his legal problems, and his gambling, and bottles in the club to look cool for his uber cool friends. I wouldn't say that he didn't do nice things for me, or for my family and friends. He did. But he did a lot of damage as well, and not just to me. He did take my parents to the Kentucky Derby once, although we booked their rooms with my credit card points, and he left me with the entire $4,000 bill when he disappeared overnight. So, I guess I bought them a trip to the Kentucky Derby. Maybe that was what she meant by him "spending everything on me and my family." I didn't even respond. I literally replied with, "Your email address has been blocked from this account and not delivered." I guess she believed it, because she never emailed me again. #tooeasy

Then the letters started coming in from H from jail. They started off nice and delusional, talking about how everything was fine and how wonderful I was. Then they slowly digressed into accusatory, blameful, rude, and degrading nonsense about how all I did was go out every day and go shopping, and now I must just be living the high life, you know, "Sipping Santana Champs because it's so crisp."

HA! I wish. Sure, I was living well compared to his prison cell, but it wasn't without pain, sacrifice, and confusion. He screwed me. I did still have my freedom, and that was something I was thankful for and terrified about at the same time. However, I did not get to go shopping and just party my face off. I didn't even have cable. #americandream

He was also the one that committed the crime. Even though I didn't wish for him to be there, one of us was a pathological liar and the other was not, so I took it with a grain of salt. I guess he didn't get it when I told him we were done, and changed my number. Delusion is your best friend when your life is full of lies.

Believe me, at this point, I was so numb to the crazy that I just felt bad for him. I really did wish him the best. But I needed to find me now. It was my time to decide not to be a victim in my life, not to be afraid of moving forward, and not to let anyone control or judge me. I had an opportunity to rebuild myself from shattered bits of glass and make a really cool mosaic out of it.

Chapter 12:

The Minute You Are Uncoupling, Everyone Else Is Coupling

One of my good friends, Larissa, from junior high and high school was getting married. I purchased my ticket long before all of this nonsense happened, so I didn't expect it to be such an ordeal. I thought to myself at the time, somewhat happy in my marriage, "Oh, I will get to see old friends, new friends, and maybe have a great time while celebrating my friend's happily ever after." Our mutual friend , Josh, actually invited me as his date to the wedding, and yes, he is of the sausage-loving sort, so don't get any sweet ideas. He called before I was supposed to fly out, and I told him everything that had happened. I asked him in confidence not to share the news, but I figured he should know what he was walking into. If I am "that person" at the wedding—you know, the broken, insane person chugging vodka and yelling about how happily ever after is a myth—I may need his support. He deserved a fair warning, but I asked him to keep it between us.

I showed up in my hometown, where I thought nobody knew, thankful for a safe haven where people weren't judging me and wouldn't ask questions. WRONG. Everyone knew. I don't know how it happened, if he told one of our friends or if the leak happened elsewhere, not that it matters now (because it really doesn't). But I digress. People were either talking about it behind my back or asking me about it to my front. Honestly, I wasn't sure which was worse. The night before the wedding, a guy I "dated" on and off for years and who completely crushed my heart, not just once but maybe seventeen times, had moved back, so we met up. I was not trying to dive into things, but it was nice to be with someone that knew me before all the awfulness and who treated me like a human being. Even if they had intimacy issues.

We spent several hours adventuring the night before the wedding, and he told me every juicy detail of what had happened in his life since I had seen him last. He asked me to do the same, but I felt like so many things had happened in the past six years that I couldn't even verbalize them. I felt like a mute. I couldn't process, so I just numbly said, "A lot." It was pretty much all I could think of. After all these years with my spouse (ex-spouse?), I couldn't think of one story to tell that defined us. Not a one. Maybe it was my intimacy issues as well. Maybe it was that I felt my number one priority was to protect myself, especially from those who eternally hurt me. I couldn't say why, but it was great to see him.

The next day, he kindly drove me and my friends to the ceremony. I won't lie to you and say that I wasn't horrified at what I might encounter. With deep breaths and Grey Goose from someone's trunk, I made it to the wedding. I kept reminding myself during the ceremony that the wedding was not about me. It was about her and her beloved, and I needed to separate my personal feelings. I did this semi-successfully. However, I can't tell you in all honesty that when I saw her in her blissful state saying those vows, I didn't feel like daggers were shooting through my veins. I just kept breathing deeply and reminding myself the day wasn't about me. It was about her. The situations were different. I avoided several emotional breakdowns and got to the reception. I was so happy for her, it was crazy. But it didn't help that half the people I ran into that actually hadn't heard the news yet kept saying things like, "Congrats on your wedding, too!" Ouch. I just responded with, "Thanks!"

Later, a girlfriend I had been close with for years confronted me about what was going on with my spouse. Needless to say, I gave her a five second version, and of course, she already knew the whole story because word traveled fast on the open plains. After I explained to her the abridged version, she let me know that she and her boyfriend had googled my spouse and that they knew he was awful from the start. I had a flashback to the time she visited me in Hollywood a few years prior, and my ex had bought her every meal and had even gotten her bottle service, but she never once accused him of being a criminal then. She had also told us how happy she was that I had met a great guy and how lucky I was. I get that hindsight is 20/20, but don't try to save face in the situation.

Then she asked me if I "knew." Yeah. Because my spouse totally said, "I committed a crime ten years ago, and I will soon be a felon. I also lie a lot. About everything." And I thought, oh, thank goodness. Let's get married. This is perfect and would just really add to the brightness of my life. I was never even the little girl who dreamed of marriage. I was extremely skeptical of it. It took a long time after we dated and got engaged to even be okay with the idea. So, let's just say I wasn't a starry-eyed lover who got blindsided here. I had a good head on my shoulders. It's just that sometimes in life, *we lose.*

To make things even weirder, I "dated" a doctor at a young age. And by young, I don't mean pedophilia; I was 18, and he was borderline Medicaid. Just kidding. He was in his 30s. He was the first person I ever hung out with regularly outside of a serious relationship/dating type situation, and the first man that ever taught me (very much by accident) the rules of casual dating. He more or less made me an expert at a young age about the games men play, and I later on mastered this. Anyhow, I thought we were a big deal at the time, and he had a lot to offer in life. I did not. I liked to party with my friends overnight and always wanted an adventure. I mean, come on, I had just finished high school. The world was at my feet.

To make a long story short, it fizzled out. I get why. He liked to go to bed early and watch the History Channel, and I liked to go out with my friends and do hood rat shit. It wasn't exactly a match made in heaven. Yet, it taught me a lot. I got drunk years later and pounded on his door before I got married, in full blackout mode, asking him what he was thinking of hanging out with someone so young. Or, at least that's what I think I said. (If you are reading this now, I'm sorry about that. It was completely inappropriate. I think.) Listen, it's not as if I wasn't a willing participant, but the older I get, the more I realize that he was an adult in that situation, and his decisions were kind of poor when it came to me.

I hadn't seen him in a long time and had virtually never run into him in our hometown. So, here I was, the morning after the wedding, and my sister picked me up from the five-star hotel (just a joke, it was a shit hole, but we stayed there kind of as a joke). We went to some new breakfast place there that used to be a Village Inn. The service was incredibly slow, and I swear it took the waitress at least 16 minutes to figure out where to seat us. When she finally did, she sat us in a low booth. Lo and behold, who was I facing not one seat away but the doc himself. I didn't want to give him the satisfaction of being curious, so I blocked his entire face with my sister's face the whole meal. He clearly said something to the guy he was with, because the guy did a 180 to stare at me for a while. Lord knows what they said, but I knew it had to be interesting. When it rains, it hails.

That night, I went out with my other childhood girlfriend and her boyfriend, and her boyfriend told me that he was planning to propose to her at the end of the month. I just watched my friend get married. I ran into a friend during her bachelor party. My other friend who was moving in with me soon was expecting a baby with her boyfriend. And here was another friend, on the brink of getting engaged. I felt like everyone was moving on with their lives, because of course they should, while I could not because of who I chose to marry. I can't dwell on it forever, but it was hard to let go of plans that we had made together, and realize that I was on my own again. No two incomes, no home buying, no baby, no white picket fence. None of it. It all turned into dust in the wind.

Chapter 13:

How to Date a Crackhead and Other Stories

I had been dating quite a bit, which I believed to be healthy and somewhat unhealthy all at the same time. I knew that eventually I would get burned out, but for the time being, it was a fun distraction and nothing serious. I was enjoying what I could about it. So, when a man at the pool named Jim asked me to go to dinner, I thought, "Sure!" We went across the street, because he remembered me mentioning to my friend at the pool that I liked a restaurant named Houston's. It was great, and on a normal day I would have been head over heels for it, but my appetite was shit at the time and I knew I wouldn't be eating much.

We walked in, and they said there was a wait. This was when my ex would have casually stepped closer to the person and sweet talked his way into the best seat in the house, but it was best in these situations not to compare one man to the next. Besides, his ability to charm and talk his way into anything probably should have been a red flag. Anyhow, we walked up to the bar while waiting for the table, and I ordered a vodka soda. Jim casually ordered a cranberry juice, and I immediately thought it was a red flag, probably AA. Where was his anniversary chip and how bad of an idea was this date? I asked him, while trying to be polite, why exactly he ordered a cranberry juice. He assured me that he was not an alcoholic, he just didn't like to drink.

As if that was somehow better. There are two types of people I do not trust in life, those who are team Jacob, and those who just choose not to drink at all. Like, hey, if you are an alcoholic, that's fine. But saying you just don't like to, is like saying I'm a tight-wad who doesn't like to have fun. It's like saying you don't like to ever eat dessert. It's America, my friends. Being an adult is hard enough. I decided to give him a break on that one, though.

We sat down, and long story short, I ordered sushi and he ordered a French dip sandwich. He didn't ask me much about myself but proceeded to tell me that he was some sort of genius Mensa type, was on a low carb diet but kept gaining weight, was in between jobs, and had a spending habit. Mind you, he was a software architect engineer or something or other, so his jobs were contract types, and he would surely land on his feet, but it was alarmingly honest. Over dessert, because he had now ruined his diet so he was going all in, he explained that he moved to Newport to find a wife and have a child, and he was in his forties so his clock was ticking. Needless to say, Jim was a very kind and honest man, and I was sure he would find his Stepford wife here no problem, but there was a clear lack of chemistry and he was a few steps ahead. Like, he was at the proposal step. So that was Jim.

Next, I went out on a date with Don, a man I had seen several times around. He drove a super nice car, not that it matters, but he had good taste and seemed to always be on the move. He was good-looking but not in a super obvious way, and from the small interactions I had had with him, he seemed intriguing. One day when I was walking my dog, he drove by me, literally did a U turn, came back, and said, "I'm sorry, but you are so my cup of tea. Please go on a date with me tonight. God has blessed me with everything that I want except a good woman." Cue the cheesy music, but hey, why not. I replied, "Don, right? We have met like three times already." Now cue the face of no recognition.

He said to be ready by six, and I canceled a friend group date in LA to meet up with Mr. Cheesy. With work and all it seemed to far a drive to deal with. After he picked me up, he asked me what I did for work, and I explained the best I could, because I really had no clue what I did half the time besides whatever it took to live. He showed me pictures of Chris Brown in the music studio and his LA friends, and told me about his company, which made a very popular new gadget that all the kids these days had. I was not understanding, and frankly nor did I really care, because I knew how this worked. He was basically my ex in a different package, an entrepreneur looking for investments, who thought it was cool that he knew lots of famous people that he paid to endorse his product to somehow hopefully turn a profit. He lived fast and would probably die young. Before we even made it to the restaurant, I knew this was a waste of time

At dinner, he ordered us both a lot of food and ate basically none of it (did I mention he was rail thin?), and left the table so many times that some guys came over from the other table, and asked what kind of idiot I was on a date with who would leave a woman like me alone so much. I agreed, but at this point everything was research and development anyway, so I rolled with it. He left constantly, couldn't stop moving around, going to the bathroom and taking cigarette breaks every two minutes. It was clear to me that he was G'd up like a motherfucker, and for those of you that don't know what this means, it is my way of saying the dude had to be railing blow like it was the 80s. He proceeded, when he was actually at the table, to talk about himself and his family and his cool friends nonstop. He asked why I was single, and I said I was dating someone who got into some legal trouble, and left it at that. I felt like he was the kind of dude who probably wasn't scared off easily. I mean, when an appetizer was a pile of snow, where did you draw the line, right?

He asked, "You didn't break up because you don't like him then, it's just because he went away?" I hated this question, because it implied that I would wait for this man, because I was so lovesick that I would hang out for 14 years like I was on the cast of *Mobwives*. "No, there were other things, but yes, that was more or less a huge factor in the breakup." He kept saying how calming I was and how he felt so on vacation and he could just relax with me. I thought to myself, lucky you, because you are bouncing around so much, I feel like I am the one on crack and I can't relax for one second.

He called a friend, who showed up and crashed the dinner. The friend, whom we will call Steve, introduced himself and his girlfriend. They got a sushi roll that they told me the chef just made up for them, and they were going to call it the SK roll for their first initials, because it was where they met. I asked if they were going to have their wedding there, and they both informed me that no they will not, but the restaurant would certainly be catering it. I then asked how long ago they met, and they both responded, "Two weeks ago."

Then Steve and my date, the tweaker, proceeded to go outside and have a cigarette together, because he had reached his limit of sitting still for all of, oh, 22 seconds. Kendra, the K in "SK," told me that it was love at first sight and they both had kids, so she and her daughter had moved into this man's house the day after they met, and how it was just meant to be. I had a feeling that one of them had done this sort of thing before, and that these things probably ended with one of them needing a restraining order. But my ex-spouse was in prison, so who was I to judge?

The men came back and this very stable couple went to the bathroom probably five times over the next few minutes. It doesn't take a rocket scientist to figure out what they were doing in there, while we were sitting in a restaurant/lounge. I mean, this wasn't EDC for goodness sake, what did they expect to do with all that energy besides go home and Ike Turner each other?

Don introduced me to lots of his friends as "his friend Danielle" and then walked away, leaving me alone with them. A man named Ken, who was clearly my father's age, said, "You are so beautiful but you are a bit too old for me." As if a man in his early sixties who spent his nights at a "restaurant/lounge" hitting on girls was a great catch. I think he expected me to have low self-esteem and throw myself at him but I just said "awesome" and walked away. He didn't like that.

Don gave me an earful after Ken hit on me, and at this point, I realized he was a complete psychopath. We headed outside for me to wait for my uber, and since I was freezing cold in my crop top dress, he offered me a t-shirt he had in the trunk of his car.

The next morning, he texted me about what a "wonderful" time he had.

I responded: "I go on a date with you and all I got out of it was this lousy t shirt."

He responded, and I cannot make this up: "Are you a hooker?"

I choked on my coffee. "Uh, no. But thanks for asking."

He said, "Well why would you say that then?"

I guessed he left his humor at his drug dealer's house. I didn't respond. Life is weird, man. Life sure is weird.

The next day, I had a blind date brunch with a completely normal human being. White-Porsche-driving, good sense of humor, lawyer, and not just any lawyer, but a partner in a firm type, who owned his home and had his life all the way together. He ate great food and was a completely perfect gentleman. Friends of mine, Kristin, and Jim, who set this up, met us down in Laguna for a lovely brunch. Jeff, my blind date, who was a long time, trusted friend of theirs, was easy to talk to, kind, and completely copacetic.

I realized in this moment that even in my adventures, which was fine for casual dating, maybe I needed to reel it in a bit. After being with those light and airy people, I needed to dial it down and away from the dark underworlds of "The Fig and Olive." It was time to maybe take a hiatus from my weeks of dating pretty much anything, and spend some time concentrating on what exactly I was looking for in life. I mean, I had experienced the full spectrum, from quiet, to doesn't drink, to looking for a wife software nerd, to the crackhead in board shorts putting money up his nose.

A few days later, a wild, older gentleman named Lenny who I'd met a few times and was so much fun, texted me and invited me for sushi at a place called Wasa in Newport. Being a sushi lover and thinking it might be nice, I told him I would meet him there. We ordered a roll each and enjoyed a nice lunch. He had ordered a chilled bottle of sauvignon blanc and offered me a glass, and in my current state, who was I to say no? I obliged the kind sir, and, two bottles later, the entire restaurant had been closed for an hour and the waiters were lying on the benches with napkins on their faces, napping before the night shift.

He explained to me that he was still married, even though he and his wife were separated. He lived in our building part-time and in a bedroom in his home part-time, where his wife and kids continued to live. They wanted to continue this arrangement for the kids. He owed most of his success as a man to his wife, so he was fine with continuing to provide for her, so what was the point in a divorce? I drank more wine. I thought I had heard it all, but I guess I was just getting started. Lenny recommended that I not drive at this point, and using the brain cells I had left, I agreed. I climbed in his convertible Mercedes, and we bumped "Bitch Better Have My Money" all the way to Gulfstream restaurant, where we drank Maker's Mark on the rocks with orange slices and smoked cigars. This is where things get blurry. However, hanging out with someone who was also in limbo and wanted nothing from you except to have a few laughs, was quite refreshing.

All I know was my bestie/new roommate ended up feeding me a sandwich and some Advil when I got home, and said that I picked up her dog Lola, and said, "No I can't, not in front of Lola," which made no sense. She also said I kept repeating, "My friend Lenny," cracking up laughing, and never finishing the sentence. Apparently, I went in to her room, asked a question, then went into it again and asked, "Was I in here recently?" And I guess I was concerned about leaving my car in the Wasa parking lot—probably a bad memory from LA—because I texted a bunch of people "I car" or other gibberish. Tom somehow showed up at my house, then valeted his car, and I ordered an Uber because he couldn't with his Blackberry (I know, who still uses those?).

He drove my car to a restaurant near my house, ordered me some food, and then took me home. As he was dropping me off and picking up his car, he told me I had been drinking too much lately, and I needed to drink less if I wanted a relationship with him, as if that was my goal in life. I replied that I had been drinking way too much that day, it was true. But it was that or hang myself from my closet coat rack, so if I needed to have a little fun to get through the night, I would. When things calmed down for me, I would scale it back. Give a girl a break. Everything was so serious with him all the time and that was the last thing I needed. Plus, I realized that if I weren't drinking as often as I was, I probably wouldn't have hung out with him this long. That may sound extremely rude and unkind, and I don't mean it to be. It was the truth though, and the truth shall set you free. I needed to set him free as well.

So, what have I learned so far about dating as a newly single gal in her late 20s? Every man is different, and they still make no freaking sense.

Chapter 14:

The Grass Isn't Always Greener, but It's Still Freakin Grass

I have learned a lot about men recently. There are the guys who are overly confident, cocky, young, and successful, who think they are better than you and will treat you like dirt. They also talk to so many women that they say emotionally forward things to you like, "Miss you babe," after your first date. They are way too comfortable after dating 1,000 women every day. Then there are the nerdy guys who never really got a lot of women, but they are now making money, so they think if they buy you enough dinners, you owe them some sexy, sexy time. There are also the 55-plus old guys who go out like it's their job, either do cocaine or provide it so the young girls will hang around, and are addicted to Lexapro and Viagra. They fuck everything that walks and do not feel sorry about it. They will play the teddy bear role to try and get you off your game, and the minute you fall for it, you will find them at your nearest shit hole bar with the town hoochie straddling them. If you try to keep up with this kind of guy, they will chew you up, spit you out, and then jump all over your regurgitated body. Then, there is the kind older man who has never settled down, clearly because something is wrong with him, and he is emotionally or mentally inept, and is now very lonely and looking for a wife. Not a specific one, just anyone in general. They will be happy to tell you this to your face over dinner.

I have dated some, all, or a combination of these guys over the past few weeks, and I must tell you, it really pissed me off. Not only do these gentleman think they hold all the cards because they have penises and a credit card, but in general, they think women are out to tie a guy down and that it is their job to duck and dodge it. I have come around not trying to do that, as I was literally just trying to get through my situation. I was lonely. I decided to treat dating like a huge experiment. I realized that I had spent every day for *years* with my spouse. We only ever spent a handful of days apart. He was my best friend, my business partner, my cheerleader, my confidant. Now I literally had no one. There is nothing like going home to a cold bed covered in dog hair, because your pug is the only physical affection you get these days and you love to cuddle with him.

I had come to the realization that I was pissed off. I was pissed off that I lost my spouse, and that he lied to me about everything and left me on my own with nothing. And I was mostly pissed, because I didn't choose this route. I didn't choose to be in this situation. I didn't want to be this girl out dating again with these loser guys who think that they are better than everyone and treat you like shit. You have to wade through so much nonsense before you even meet someone you even remotely want to be around. I used to feel like a classy woman and I was treated like one. Now there was no controlling how these people treated me. Sure, I didn't have to be around them or go out with them again, but some of the stuff people say to a woman is astounding to me, the things they think are acceptable or that you will put up with. I didn't choose this.

I also noticed that people treated me differently after hearing my story. The first question everyone asked when they heard about my situation or that my ex and I weren't together was, "Are you moving home?" or "Are you still in SoCal?" as if I couldn't live here without a husband. I don't understand that. I guess it was a valid question, but I was sick of people thinking the only reason a girl could stay in a nice place was if a guy was paying her way to do so. I find that to be completely insulting.

Our couple friends also didn't invite me places anymore either. Like, literally. I guess I was not that cool without my sidekick. For business purposes, my associates used to invite us out, but they didn't as much anymore. H used to be such a good time, so great with people, to the point where I started taking a backseat to him and his exuberant self. I used to be super fun, and I didn't feel like I was as much anymore, after so many years of accommodating his need to shine. I had to figure out how to be me again. Not the me that I used to be, but the new me who I was now. I didn't like being alone at night. I didn't like being alone during the day. The more I was alone, the more I thought. The more I thought, the more depressed I became. The more depressed I became, the more panicked I got, and the deeper I went down the rabbit hole.

I continued to sell real estate with Paula, and while that had been great, I just felt that I was so out of control of my future. I was not in control of how much money I made. I was not in control of when I worked. If she decided we were stopping somewhere during the day, we were stopping somewhere during the day, which was most days during work. What day was a workday? Every day. I couldn't plan, I couldn't schedule. When I asked questions about how the company worked, how I'd like to make more, and how the commissions didn't make sense, her response was that I needed to work more, maybe get a desk job. Most people wouldn't have put up with it for so long, but at the time I didn't have a lot of options. My brain wasn't working right. I wasn't working right.

I just needed the time, energy, and effort to grow my own business. I needed to do it. I had to do it. I didn't know any other way. I knew that the people I met through my ex were some of the best, and some were the worst. It wasn't all bad. He showed me the world. He showed me how to believe in myself (and, yes, eventually doubt myself). I had a glimmer of hope for how I could make life what I wanted. I didn't have any other options. I saw no other way, and there wasn't anything else I wanted to do with my life. It made sense to me now that my purpose might be to help other people avoid the situation I was in now. How did I get from point A to point B? Did I need to take the time for meditation, contemplation, and reflection? Sure, I probably did. I also knew that I had bills that needed to be paid, and a lease that was up in two-and-a-half months, so I kind of didn't have the time and luxury of that.

Lord, Universe, Dolly Parton? If you are there, please watch over me. I need you now more than ever.

Chapter 15:

How to Convince Your Parents You Are Suicidal and Date Your Ex's Friends

First off, let's get one thing straight. I really wouldn't date my ex's friends. I don't think. However, once I had a business meeting with H and his friend who I know pretty well, who brought along a friend named Manny. Now, Manny was not only a strikingly handsome man, but he also was sharply dressed, intelligent, and into nutrition. I was very into nutrition as well, though you wouldn't be able to tell from my current state at the time. And by that, I mean I hadn't been caring for myself the way I should. On to that later.

My ex didn't introduce me as his wife for whatever reason. I guess he thought it would seem more professional, since he was always putting on some sort of appearance. Anyhow, this Manny and I had an instant connection. I was married, so I didn't think much of it, but he kind of flirted and locked eyes with me and seemed very intrigued in getting to know me better. Obviously, he left after and didn't ask for my number or anything, and I'm sure my ex and my friend told him later that I was married (if he even brought it up). I remembered Manny saying where he lived at the time, which was literally about two or three blocks from where I lived, and I thought it was weird I had never run into him before. And I never ran into him afterward, either. Until recently.

I was leaving our local pho restaurant that I have been to probably 50 times, and as I walked out, I saw a gorgeous dog being held by his owner, who was in a circle chatting with people. I decided it would be a good idea to sashay over and say, "Can I pet your dog?" The man seemed slightly taken aback but said, "Sure." I pet the dog and looked up… "Manny?" No. Freaking. Way.

Basically, I reminded him that we had met through our mutual friend, although I felt like he never really put two and two together. He asked if I had his number, and I said no. He put his number into my phone, and we texted back and forth a few times. He asked me out for pho finally, which I thought was a copout because the pho restaurant was not really the best date spot. It was more of our local "Cheers" hangout, but perhaps he was trying to take me somewhere he knew I would like. I agreed to go with him in two days, and within an hour he canceled because he had to go to LA All this told me was that Manny knew he was cool and he didn't log our pending date as super important. I only know this because I canceled dates I was not thrilled about for better ones all the time. Sorry if you are reading this, and I cancelled our date.

So, the next few times Manny tried to schedule a date with me, I was "busy." After a while, he went from offering me a Thursday position to offering a Saturday night date slot. Instead of taking me to pho, we had upgraded to a fancy place, my favorite mussels restaurant. Oddly enough, I had never been there up until a few months ago, and now this was the third date of mine to take me to such an establishment. We sat and ate dinner, and the conversation flowing freely. I tried not to drink too much as I didn't want to get sloppy with Mr. Normal over here. I wore the earrings my mother gave me on my wedding day that I never got a chance to wear. I also felt unhealthy, uncomfortable, not like myself. I'd never felt less confident in my life.

Manny was a perfect gentleman. A strange man came up, completely wasted, and spoke gibberish to us and proceeded to sniff the back of Manny's neck. Manny handled it all like a pro. Then, the drunk man proceeded to touch my shoulder, and Manny proceeded to politely remove his hand and asked if he minded moving on his way, as we were kind of trying to have a conversation. He ordered us some food, told me some great stories, drove me home, opened the door for me to get out and hugged me before I walked inside. Had I just met a normal person? I mean he was 39 and unmarried, didn't drink, and loved his mother and sister. He was a former professional athlete and did a lot of charity work for kids. Something must be wrong with him.

A few days later, I was in a slump. When I say that, I don't mean, oh wow I am feeling down, but, like, for real, I was thinking back on my life, the dreams that I had, and the life I thought I would be leading at this point. I was the 18-year-old girl who made vision boards, read *The Success Principles* 57 times in a row, and meticulously mapped out where she wanted life to go. Not in a psycho way, but in a "let's put some plans into action and then make decisions to help life guide us" type of way. Okay, so maybe meticulously pseudo-psycho. My mom was a sheriff. I did background checks on my ex. I went through his stuff. So, if you are reading this and think I didn't do my homework, sorry to tell you, I did. And then some. It could happen to anyone.

So, the fact that I ended up in this position in my late 20s was odd to me. I didn't make rash decisions saying, "Well, screw it." I had made well thought-out, responsible, adult decisions. Unfortunately, as the saying goes, "Life is what happens when you are busy making other plans." I'm not sugar coating when I say that my husband made my existence real. He actually cared what happened to me every day (or seemingly). When someone shares every intimate moment with you for years, and you tell them all the nuances of your life, suddenly you feel invisible without that reflection. To say that it was difficult would be putting it mildly.

I had a lot of hard relationships before this one. To say that I held men at arm's length would be an understatement. I never let anyone in. The fact that I even let him near me took YEARS. I mean it. He asked me to move in with him forever before I even considered it. He asked me to marry him, and I said yes without hesitation, but then I hesitated for several years before I would even plan our wedding with him. I would ask and he would hesitate, and I was happy with that. It's no surprise my bridal party walked down the aisle to "Bittersweet Symphony." That's not a joke. I picked it myself.

After spending time thinking about all of these things, I laid on my bed one afternoon, and even though I had had my moments in the past, I had remained rather unscathed up until this particular moment. My phone rang, and just as the severity of the situation really hit me, I picked up the phone. It was my mom. I usually loved talking to her, but lately, I could almost hear the pain and uncertainty in her voice of whether or not I was going to pull through this. She has always believed in me more than anyone, so that scared the shit out of me. Instead of avoiding her, I felt that maybe she could cheer me up when I was down, like she used to, and I answered. Skipping to the important moments:

Mom: "So I think you should just come home for a while."

Me: "Sure, Mom, that will just be the icing on the cake. I've fought so hard to stay here, now I just give up and come home?"

Mom: "Why not? You can always go back."

Me: "Okay, so I go back just to come here and start all over again like I did years ago? That would suck. I will be miserable there."

Mom: "Well, Dani, you are miserable there."

Me: "Yeah, I know. Thanks."

Mom: "Things don't seem like they are working out that well for you."

Me: "Yes, I get it Mom. My life sucks. I understand."

Mom: "So, come home."

Me: "What would I even do there? I would rather live in my car here."

Mom: "You could do anything here! Or do nothing! Build a business, whatever you want."

Me: "Mom. I would rather be a stripper here and live in my car. If I come home, I will literally ice myself. I will jump off the roof of your house. I can't do it." I got teary-eyed. I obviously thought she knew I wasn't going to ice myself or strip. I'd said this to her before in conversations, albeit in a better mood, but I think she knew my humor by now. However, I was more upset than usual. I was sure she could hear it in my voice. We hung up.

My phone rang again. It was my sister Cassidy. "Are you okay?"

Me: "Yeah I'm fine. Let me guess, did you just talk to Mom?"

Cassidy: "Yeah, she seems worried about you."

Me: "Oh lord. I just told her I was going to ice myself. I didn't think that she would take it seriously."

Cassidy: "You have said crazier things. Anyway, I'm supposed to call and check on you periodically from now on and make sure you aren't suicidal."

So now I am accidentally and undeservingly on suicide watch. Or perhaps semi-deservingly.

Chapter 16:
The $200,000 Baby

*T*was out showing property one day with my coworker, Paula, when she randomly broke off from me, which I knew meant she was showing property she didn't want to split commission on and that was fine. They were her clients. But normally we were a dynamic duo. I didn't mind, so I got to work on other tasks. After a while, I started getting anxious and gave her a ring to see if she'd like to have a late afternoon lunch. Most of my work was done, and I didn't feel like sitting at home alone listening to the sound of my dog snoring.

Paula said sure, she would meet for lunch, but just a warning, she rolled her ankle showing a property, so she wasn't walking well. We decided to go to lunch in Fashion Island. A restaurant there had a great rose and a wonderful salad. She picked me up, and I noticed some scrapes on her arm. I figured she was being dramatic about the ankle roll until we actually got to Fashion Island. Getting out the car, I realized that Paula could literally not walk. She was wearing kitten-ish wedge heels, and hobbling along the best she could, but I had to hold her arm and help her. We parked maybe 20 feet from the restaurant entrance, and I would guess it took us a good 15 minutes to get to the door.

I suggested several times that we skip lunch and take her somewhere more fitting. For instance, I dunno, a hospital? Paula refused. I called my mom, because she is a genius with human body things, (maybe because she has one, I'm not sure), and after relaying to Paula several questions, my mom told me that it was probably just severely sprained and to stay off it, elevate it, and take some medication for the swelling. Paula told me that wine was her medication, and we were going to enjoy our lunch, so that was that.

When you walk into the restaurant, it has a huge, horseshoe-shaped bar and tables around the outskirts. The table wait time is pretty long during peak hours, so it's usually easier to grab some bar seats if you can. There was an open gap at the bar where some stools had been moved, so I borrowed a chair from a high top table nearby that only had two people at a four top, thinking that Paula needed a freaking chair before her foot turned into a hot air balloon. The hostess watched me move the barstool all the way over to the bar before coming over and removing it from my hands like a toddler. "I'm sorry, we don't allow people to move the chairs from tables. If you can't find a chair at the bar, it means they are all taken."

"Okay, I understand, but someone obviously took some chairs FROM the bar, because there are at least two or three missing from that area. So, if you would like paying customers, one of which is injured, to STAND at your friggin' bar, while there are the exact same empty chairs being unused that could seat paying customers, I totally get it. That makes perfect sense to me. Thank you for your help." She rolled her eyes at me and walked away. A chair finally opened up on the left side of the horseshoe shape, and we bum-rushed (okay, I bum-rushed, Paula limped like a one-legged person) over to snatch it. I let Paula take the chair, because she obviously needed it. At this point, I was surprised she wasn't requesting a bottle of Everclear straight. Her foot looked gnarly. There was a very good-looking gentleman next to me, and he stood from his chair and offered it to me. I explained that there was no need, I really just wanted Paula to have a seat, given her current condition, and I knew these seats were hard to come by. He didn't care. He insisted. I sat.

We ordered glasses of rosé, some sort of wine they served that Paula loved, and this man stated that it should be put on his tab. Classy. He also had an accent and challenged us to guess where it was from. I already knew he was South African, because one of my first bosses in LA had the same accent, but most people would guess Australian since they sound similar. So, he let us guess, and Paula said, "Australian?" I said, "Hmmm. Let me think. South African." He smiled and said, "Wow! You are so right!"

He kept ordering more rosé for us and beers for himself. Our late, casual lunch turned into a three-hour festivity. I kept turning down glasses of wine, but they somehow kept being refilled. I tried to explain that I knew my limits and that I appreciated it, but really, I didn't need more. They just kept coming, not even when they were empty. Like, he kept recommending the bartender "freshen them."

We got on the subject of relationships, and this man, who I later learned was named "Scott," started saying how he wasn't sure he believed in marriage or love for that matter, but his mom was some sort of psychologist guru. I could tell that someone talking this way must have had his heart severely broken and his mom had tried to science the shit out of him. Whatever works. Life is hard and people get hurt, but man up and keep your balls together.

Paula was interested in this and kept asking him why he said that. He noticed Paula's engagement ring and asked her about it. She came up with some nonsense about how she wasn't sure she needed marriage either, it was just a piece of paper. They went on and on dissing marriage and love in some sort of pseudo-jaded psycho realization. Paula proceeded to tell him about my marriage and what happened, as if it was somehow her story to tell. I realized some time ago that when people don't have a lot to speak about their own lives, they like to interject with yours.

Scott mentioned that he looks at relationships like a business decision. He said that if a woman he is with gets pregnant, she should be compensated for the time she takes off work. Expenses should be paid. Her body will change. This should all be compensated for. Paula told him how smart she thought this was. I minded my business for a while and sipped on my wine, and let this go on for some time. I finally jumped in. "Okay. That's it. Have either of you ever been married before?" They looked at me as if a raccoon just popped up and joined the conversation. Both of them separately mumbled, "Well, no. Never married before."

I lost it at this point. "Okay, great. So here we are having a conversation, and the fact is neither of you has been fucking married. So, let me tell you, it is different. It's not a piece of paper. It's a merger of two lives and you are making a commitment to one another. You do it in front of your friends and family. It should be sacred, and, God-dammit, it is important. So, if you don't want to get married, then don't. But don't sit here and piss on marriage when you know nothing about it because you are jaded and pissed off. Marriage isn't the problem, people are the problem!"

They stared. Paula made a comment. "Well, I just don't know why it's necessary. Yours didn't turn out that well, and I'm just not sure if a person needs to get married." Steam rolled off me. To this day, I am still embarrassed by what happened next. "No, Paula, you want to get married. You would love to get married. You just don't want to get married to the man you're with because he has his own problems. You tell me all the time you love marriage and you want to be married. So, don't tell me marriage is the problem. Your issues with him are the motherfucking problem." Paula went to the restroom. She suggested we leave. "Scott paid for the tab, which listed a total of 14 rosés between us. He'd had more Modelos than should physically be possible, but I didn't judge and couldn't read the exact amount. Let's just say he had been there for quite some time before we arrived.

A few days later, I surprisingly got a text from Scott I was confused why, after all the punishment and crazy shit I did, this man would text me. He was distinguished, dressed well, and clearly had money, so why would he pursue someone so abrupt? Who knows. He invited me to a restaurant called Sol. I said sure, I'll meet you after finishing up with work. I took an Uber to Sol, because I knew I would have at least one drink, and ain't nobody need a DUI these days. I walked in and found him at the bar, drinking, what else, a Modelo. He asked if I'd like a margarita, but I informed him that was probably too much for me. I was trying to take it easy. I ordered a white wine, and we chatted.

He told me that I was in the prime of my life, and that I obviously didn't take it for granted. He talked to me about how captivating I was and how he thought that was great. I agreed. I do have a good spirit and a good attitude. I was just not operating at 100 percent of my usual self, so I was always confused that people found me interesting at this point in my life. Plus, I knew it was probably laced with some form of expectation. What was he trying to gain from his compliments? I wished I was more oblivious. The bartender literally refused to serve him any more beers, because he had had approximately 11. I had been there for 20 minutes. How long had he been at this establishment? The guy seemed sober as a gopher, which was confusing, but he was clearly a professional. He negotiated that he would have one water, and the bartender agreed to give him one more beer if he drank the water. He drank his water and beer and then asked if I'd like to go to the Balboa Bay Club. It was a classy place, so I felt like there wasn't much trouble we could get in to there.

We went outside, and he paid the valet to keep his car overnight. I found that responsible, but it was some sort of BMW smart car, which was weird because he was stylish and it didn't fit his MO. Maybe he just didn't care. Neither did I really. I just found it an odd choice for his personality type. Anyhow, we Ubered to the Balboa Bay Club, had more drinks at the bar, and ordered some appetizers. I was thrilled about this, because I needed some kind of sustenance. Finally, he got deep with me and told me that he didn't look for much when he met a woman these days, as far as relationships and marriage go. He informed me that he looked at a woman, and made a decision, "Could I have a baby with this woman?" and if the answer was yes, he decided to get to know her better.

You would think this would be a sweet and nostalgic romance story, but you would be wrong. He proceeded to ask me if I would want to have a baby. I responded with, "Yes, someday. I really would like to be a mom. I like to work though, and I'd like to wait until I can give my child a really good life." I'm not sure how he phrased it, but he more or less told me that if I would be interested in having a baby with him, and of course, no need to decide now (?), he would pay me $200,000. I literally inhaled my drink up my nose and coughed. This had to be a joke, right?

I asked him why the hell he has to pay people to have his kids. He responded, "I don't have to pay for anyone to have my kids. I am just not sure I am a one-woman kind of man. I also realize that having a baby is a huge time commitment for a woman with work, with her body and with her time energy and effort. I figure this will make you comfortable and make sure the child is well taken care of." I couldn't comprehend this, but my version of a perfect love story and doing things "the right way" hadn't panned out well for me, so I was only conversationally curious about his lifestyle choice. He asked me again, "Do you think that is something you could handle?"

I responded, "Listen. If I have a baby with someone, I am pretty sure I would want them involved. I would want a partner. I would want the help. Not a paycheck." His response killed me.

"Well, what if I bought you a house on Balboa Island, got you two nannies, and made sure you had more money than you would ever need to live? Would you consider it then?" I had no response to this. It was so beyond my realm of normal that I just didn't respond.

"Why have you come up with this?" I asked, honestly wanting to know the answer. He said he had to use the restroom. I ordered an Uber, walked out, got in the car, and headed home. He texted and called me. I shut my phone off and went to sleep. The next day, I woke up to a text: "I am sorry if I was too forward. It was such a pleasure getting to know you, and I hope I didn't ruin my chance to get to know you more in the future."

???????

And then I realized he had pulled a leave-behind-sunglasses-in-purse move. When did men start doing the leave-behind? I looked at the sunglasses and figured if he could afford to pay 200 grand for a woman to birth his child, he clearly could afford another pair. I chucked them in the trash and went for a run to clear my head.

Chapter 17:
Birthday Boy

I met a new guy. I know, exhausting keeping up with me at this point. However, I didn't do it on purpose. And between the whirlwind of my life after marrying a sociopath conman, handling our bills by myself, and dealing with a divorce on my own, who can keep up anyway? My neighbor D invited me out with him and his girlfriend to our mutual friend's birthday party. Being that I had nothing to do that day, I decided to go. I had taken some time off from going out, not because I didn't like to, but because I literally felt like life was too exhausting to keep up with. I couldn't cope. I didn't feel like myself, and I'd had a few odd nights. I was starting to view humanity in a dark and dingy manner, and I realized it was probably a good idea to be late to the party for a while or to just not show up at all.

However, Hesh, our friend whose birthday we were celebrating, was super cool, and I knew I'd have fun. They also invited me to the pre-party at D's, and we were all going to take a limo together. I obliged, because it was easy, and I wore the easiest dress I could find that took the least amount of work. It happened to be a red halter dress I'd bought years before. I wouldn't say I felt sexy in it, but it was the best case scenario with what I was working with. Zero effort involved. It was go time.

We all got in the limo and went out to Aqua, a local nightclub that was the weirdest fucking place on the planet. It was like Miami circa 1989 with a lot of cougars who'd had bad plastic surgery, as well as bottle rats just trying to find a free drink. No offense, I mean, believe me, I chased free drinks when I was 19 to about 22. But, past that age, you should be more selective about what you are drinking, not to mention at least be able to afford two drinks and get yourself drunk enough to find a nice, lonely man to buy you a third and fourth of your own selection. Just my observation. Anyhow, the crowd that night was super awkward. I looked around at a place I used to go to with my husband and used to find non-threatening and fun. Now, all I could see literally was a sea of sharks and chewed up minnows. I was fresh bait. Not as fun on the other side of things.

I decided to leave our bottle service tables (all three of them) behind the DJ booth and wander around, because I was bored. Life must have more to offer than this. I ran into a few friends and ended up going outside to get some fresh air before I had a full-blown depression panic attack. These two men sauntered up to me and keep commenting on how amazing my red dress was, and; "What made me wear the red dress tonight?" They interrupted my mid-midlife crisis and got me laughing. Okay. I didn't have the heart to tell them it was the only thing I easily found to put on and really didn't put any effort into it, but they seemed impressed, so I let it go. One of them was very good-looking and the other was his hysterical friend. They talked me up. We talked shit. They offered to buy me a drink, and I said sure! The hot one, who we will call "Sir," told the bartender, "She wore the red dress, get her whatever she wants."

Well, I ordered myself a vodka soda, and he ordered a Corona. I saw a random guy friend across the way and waved at him. He ended up paying for the drinks, and awkwardly asked me out again (he had proposed at a bar once kind of jokingly in the past). I declined. I'm not sure Sir noticed. The bartender gave us our drinks, and he went back to his group of friends. I handed Sir his Corona and proceeded to go back to chatting with him and his friend Matt. Sir went on about how he wanted them to play his favorite song and how I would never know what it was. I wouldn't guess it in a million years.

I said, "Well what could it be?"

He said, "It's by e-40."

I said, "You mean 'Choices'? Yep. Nope," reciting part of the lyrics.

He seemed impressed. I found it nostalgic, because I had been listening to it on repeat for three weeks straight. He was slightly aloof but incredibly sexy. My friends kept walking by and trying to lure me back to the table, but these guys seemed super fun and different from the rest of the crowd, so I stuck around. We talked about the *Wolf of Wall Street,* which I had watched the last three nights in a row, and they started calling me "The Duchess." They then tried to inform me I was the hottest girl there, at which point I just assumed that either they were shit-canned or thought that I was inept enough to believe such smooth-talking nonsense. Unfortunately, I was divorcing the smoothest talking liar on the planet. At this point, I understood all the games.

Matt disappeared at some point with some girl he ran into from high school. Sir and I started dancing, and suddenly, the lights awkwardly turned out. The party was over. Matt returned and tried to order a shot, but they weren't serving anymore, so he disappeared again with the high school girl. Sir turned to me and said, with mouth-chewing action, "I need food. Want to get some?" and we went outside to try to get an Uber to go find food, which meant I was ditching my party and their limo service, but hey, I figured they were all couples, what did they care?

The only after-hours spot for food nearby was IHOP. So, there I was at 2 AM, sitting in a booth at the International House of Pancakes, wearing Louboutins, chatting with Sir. He was very different from anyone I had met before. I couldn't quite put my finger on it. He seemed slightly moody and kind of unassuming, which I found attractive. We both ordered ham and cheese egg something sandwiches. He asked if it was okay if he sat next to me, which was cute. Most guys these days just try to invite themselves into your vagina without so much as a shared gesture, so I thought it was cheeky. He paid the check and said, "Well, where can we go? My car and all my stuff is at my buddy's house and I don't have any way to get into my place."

Um. Was this a line? He seemed like he knew how to play the game better than that. I played along. It was well past 2 AM, so it wasn't as if we were going to another club. My neighbor D and all my friends went to an after-hours spot, and I suggested we meet up with everyone there. He declined. I said, "Well, I live down the street, so I guess we can go there? You are welcome to stay, but if you are a weird serial killer, be warned, I have no problem murdering you." Plus, I thought if this was one of those, "Let's go to my house and watch a 'movie' type of plays," then, my friend, you got a new thing coming to you.

Now, I had never really brought a guy to my home like this, especially since I had roommates now. But his friend had left him behind and all of his stuff was at his friend's house, so I figured, what the hell. He seemed genuine and kind, and in a hard spot. Plus, I was experimenting. He offered to sleep on the couch, which was kind, but I said it was okay if he wanted to sleep in the bed. He asked if he could take his pants off and assured me he would be a proper gentleman, which I slightly didn't believe, but conceded, to see where he thought he was going with this.

I had a dream that night that I dropped him off at his house, and that he called me later and I could hear him with a lady in the background and a crying baby. In my dream, he had a wife and a child. I woke up in a cold sweat. I didn't sleep well because one, I was sleeping in my own guest room, and two, there was a strange man in my bed. Yet, he was indeed a perfect gentleman.

In the morning, I noticed he had a tattoo on his arm of a child. "Who is that?" He told me, "That's me when I was younger." I didn't respond, but I could tell he was lying, plus he didn't seem ridiculous enough to have his younger self emblazoned on his arm for life. I decided to let it go. He asked if I wanted to get breakfast, and I said sure, not knowing how good of an idea this was going to be, but at this point, he seemed pretty great. I think he was just pacifying me to burn time, but hey, we would see what happened. A girl's gotta eat. We went to breakfast at some place in Newport, a little diner that Sir loved. Our waitress kept talking to me about her child. Sir seemed super interested in what age the kid was and how all of that was going. I found this endearing. He then asked if he should Uber to his friend's house in Huntington Beach, which I know nothing about, but being kind, I offered to take him. He had me drop him off, and I assumed I would never hear from this guy again.

He texted me the next day and asked if I would like to go see a movie. I was slightly amused, because nobody really invites people on movie dates anymore. He asked what I wanted to see, and my mom kept telling me I had to see *Trainwreck* with Amy Schumer, because I was basically Amy Schumer and the movie was pretty much written for me. I decided this was a good movie for us to go see. We went to R + D Kitchen, had dinner, and then went to the movie. He ordered a water at dinner, and then another one at the movie, which I thought was odd. During the movie, he kept touching something in his sock, and at one point, he poured his cup of water out, thinking he was being sneaky. He also kept putting something in his mouth, which I found odd. I even think I heard some sort of biting.

Fuck. This guy was totally on some sort of prescription pills. He seemed distant, his eyes seemed slightly odd all night, and now he was sneaking some shit in the movie. He wasn't drinking, although he didn't claim to "not drink," so at this point, yeah, I had pretty much narrowed down that he did some sort of pills. "Great," I thought, "Here we go again." The movie was slow and awkward. It was like watching paint dry. We left. I hated the movie. He said he didn't like the movie either. We got back to my house (How did we end up here again? Most men like to go to their places.) I confronted him about the pill thing.

"So, dude. What exactly were you doing in the movie? I know you were hiding something."

"Oh, well, I don't want to tell you," he responded.

"Are you on pills or something? I know you were doing something."

"Okay. I chew tobacco."

"Oh, that's all? Can I have some?" I responded. I was from Wyoming, for goodness sake. Where I grew up, everyone chewed tobacco.

The next day, we went out for dinner and he seemed nervous. Not in a like "oh, a new girl! Let's impress her" sort of way, but like an "announce the death of a family member" kind of way.

He started the conversation point blank. "Do you like kids?"

I wondered in what sort of way. Was I a child molester, did he mean? Or did I want to have kids, like tonight? Was I being offered money to have one (again)? Did I want them someday? Or, did I like them in general? Let's just say it could have been taken a lot of ways.

"Yeah, I like kids," I said, while casually drinking a glass of wine.

"I have a three-year-old."

Gulp. "Oh. Okay. What's his name?"

He explained to me about his son and how he was getting divorced because his ex-wife was cheating on him. He was wishy-washy about the timing, but it seemed it was only about five to six months ago, which was funny, because so was mine. His child tattoo made sense now, not that I didn't have an inkling. I found out later his divorce was not final. So, technically, my dream was correct. Guy had a child and a "wife."

Now, all of this should have worried me, especially because he never asked me questions about myself, and most things we did discuss were about him, but I let it go because I was too out of energy in life to make a big deal out of it. The more we hung out, the more I liked him, but his soon-to-be ex-wife texted him about 100 times a day. Sure, I could believe that the texts were about the kid, if I were born in a barn and dumb as a pile of rocks. As a child of divorce, and being raised around lots of other people who have been divorced, and going through one (sorta) myself, I would have to say that their relationship was odd. They were obviously leaning on each other for emotional support in some way, and it was hard to lose that connection when you are co-parenting from afar and spawned a child together.

This fact alone kept me from taking it too seriously. I realized that I would like to, but I'm pretty sure they were still tied up in something. Would they get back together? Could be drama. I was also probably not in the most positive state of mind, to be with a man who was newly divorced, since I was as well. Or, not even divorced, since I guess he was still legally married at this point. I couldn't really judge him for it, as these things take time, but I didn't want to do something out of ease and comfort rather than passion. And everyone deserves a little passion in life. We seemed to be in similar states of mind, which made it work between us, but I just didn't want to be taken for granted or pay for someone else's mistakes.

Sir invited me over to his place for the first time, and I took an Uber there. I told my Uber driver all about Sir, because Uber drivers were the new free therapists, just like hairdressers used to be. She told me I should just go for it. I arrived at Sir's house, and he was on their patio having a glass of whiskey. I sat down, and he brought me some wine. I didn't know exactly how comfortable I was supposed to be here. All of the sudden, I heard, "Daddy! Daddy! Where are you?" and he booked it inside to tend to the child. He was gone for about 10 minutes or so, and returned. We chatted for a bit.

"Daddy?!" He went back inside. This cycle continued about three more times before I asked him if I should just go. Not that I minded he was tending to his child, it was pretty attractive actually, but I just felt in the way at this point. He explained that his kid's birthday was the next morning and he was used to sleeping with Sir, so the kid was more amped up than usual, and thank you so much for coming over, but it was more or less time to Uber home.

I heard once more, "Daddy, daddy!' and off he went again. I didn't know if I should leave this time or stay to say goodbye. It was an awkward, in-between moment. Then, he came out, holding his half-asleep son and introduced us. "This is Danielle." I didn't know what else to say. "Pound it." And I offered a fist up. He obliged and off they went back upstairs. Had I just meet this guy's kid? I didn't know how to feel about it. He came back down and said goodbye so I could get my Uber home, and off I rode into the Orange County darkness.

Chapter 18:

How to Burn Your Old Life Down

*A*fter several months surviving on my own, and selling everything of value just to get by, and my friends/bosses at my real estate work screwing me over financially, I started to panic. I had sold my wedding ring. I had been working nonstop. I was exhausted. I had had no time to process anything. I got letters from my soon-to-be ex-husband constantly. I would get barrages of emails, texts, letters. Our place reminded me of him. Everywhere I went there were memories, haunting me like a bad dream. I had to change my phone number more times than I would like to admit, because he somehow found it and repeatedly called. He owed me a lot of money, got some back from taxes, and sent it to his mother instead. Awesome.

So, I was stressed. Like, beyond stressed. Like, so stressed I couldn't even function. You know it's bad when your phone ringing causes you to almost have a mental breakdown. The funny part is when you are stressed, and people yell at you for being stressed, because they think it's about them. It's like, um, no, not all of the world revolves around you. Believe me, I wish it did, then I would have less responsibility.

After a long talk with my cousin, and several sleepless nights, I realized that if I continued down this path around these people, I was never going to heal correctly. It was like a broken bone. If it didn't get set right, it would never heal completely. So, I needed to get set right. Yes, I am referring to myself as a broken bone. I also had been so focused on just surviving that I hadn't had a lot of time or perspective to think clearly. I spent all of my time worried about making money, making sure my friends weren't mad at me, taking care of my divorce, putting out all of my ex's fires, trying not to disappoint everyone, and just making it through the day in general.

I realized that if I didn't find out how to make a bunch of money quickly so I could relax a little, I probably needed to go home to the middle of nowhere and just take it easy for a bit. Like a sabbatical. This was the worst-case scenario for me. I started to brainstorm the best ways to make fast cash, you know, the legal way. Drug dealing and breaking into cars were out, my hands are too delicate for all that. Plus, I didn't want to end up cellmates with my ex.

I started by looking around at people who made a lot of money and cruising Craigslist. As a female, here are the plethora of awesome options I came across:

A "high-class escort service," where you "aren't required to do anything you don't want to do." Yeah, right. They always say that. It basically means, "We can't require you to bang people, but if you don't, you won't get clients, then you won't get paid." Not going to work for me.

Webcam modeling. These girls are basically personal, online porn stars, and to make any sort of money, you are kind of at the whim of these men who pay you for personal shows, and you more or less have to do what they ask. Oh yeah, and masturbate. A lot. No thank you.

Start a medical marijuana farm. I know nothing about marijuana. I am also too nice sometimes. I'd probably believe people's sob stories and give it away for free, or end up murdering all my plants. (I suck at keeping plants alive.) Plus, it would take too long. So, that was out.

I guess I could have that dude's baby for 200k and a house. That should give me some time to relax. But no, I could never do it. Fuck having morals and integrity and dignity. People make it out to be so cool. It's not. It just means it makes life that much harder, which I know will make it easier in the long run. It's like, do you want Plan A or Plan B? (HA! Not that Plan B. Nice try, though)

Plan A: Make things easier now but much harder in the long run.

Plan B: Make things much harder now but easier in the long run.

Thanks, Mom and Dad, for actually raising me correctly. I guess I was going to my hometown in Wyoming, the one place I always promised myself I would never, ever go back to. But I could take a month off work, relax in peace and quiet, and actually process my life crumbling down. I called my cousin T and she said, "You'll need someone there with you when you leave, even though it's temporary. I'll fly out and we'll drive back together, so you can bring your stuff!" This was music to my ears. My lease was up on my apartment, so I would just sell what I could and toss the rest, leave with a clean slate, and return and start over. Over, over. Again.

Sir tried to get me to stay and find a place with him, but I didn't want to move in with someone just because it was convenient. I wanted him to want to move in together because he actually liked me. And I'd just done the whole move-out-the-person's-stuff thing. Alone. So had he. Was it worth doing again? What if it didn't work out? We were spending a lot of time together, but I couldn't ever figure out if he wanted me as a partner passionately with wild abandon, or if it was just "easy, so why not."

I got off the phone and looked around my apartment. I had years of accumulated shit from my life in California, as well as years before that living in other places. I also had my ex's leftover things: files, a Range Rover he had given me that I couldn't sell (because of a lien on the title from him, thanks a bunch), two beds, dressers, couches, four flat screen TVs, a dining room set, a computer desk, closets full of stuff, and Lord knows what else. So, my next thought was, how the hell am I going to get all this shit out of here by the first? Which is literally days away. Not weeks. Not even *a* week. DAYS.

I started posting my things on Craigslist for dirt cheap. My furniture was practically brand new. I had an $800 coffee table. I posted it for $200. My bed set was worth God knows what. I listed it for pennies on the dollar. Time was of the essence. I realized I could either be paid something for other people to come take my shit, or I could pay movers to come throw it in the trash. After pretty much zero bites on the CL, I texted a friend and she suggested an app called "Offer Up." She warned me that I probably wouldn't get what I paid for the items, but at least it was something. I told her that I was already taking a loss, so I was hip with it. I posted my things on there, and, lo and behold, offers started coming through.

The first day, I sold my patio set and my coffee table, which of all things hurt the most to part with. I had lusted after it for a year and my parents bought it for me as a wedding gift. It was a total surprise, and I cherished it every moment I spent with it. Everything else was easy to be unattached to; they were like old fragments of a life that wasn't mine anymore. I felt nothing as they were hauled off. Almost relief even.

Over the next few days, pieces of my furniture sold here and there. By the time my cousin came, I still had both beds, three dressers, and some other heavy odds and ends furniture items. It was Wednesday evening when I picked her up from the airport, and we decided to head out Saturday. That way, we could spend Saturday and Sunday in Vegas, and be back in Wyoming by Monday, dropping her off in Colorado in time to start her new job on Tuesday. Wednesday night, we went out to eat with Sir, the man with the baby. He barely said two words to my cousin besides, "Hi, nice to meet you." He was talkative with me, but he seemed super shy around her.

We headed to Javier's because I wanted to show my cousin a true Orange County haunt, and the entire drive there he was practically silent. I didn't know if he was being a mute because he was nervous, or if he really just didn't like to fucking talk. He usually made conversation. Not that he was huge on it, but he put in an effort most the time. T told me later that she hated him almost immediately and that he was miserable and needy, and only wanted to be near me because I was strength and he could sense that I was wounded but rebuilding, and he wanted to lean on me. I shrugged. He told me he thought she needed attention and he didn't want to give it to her.

We finished dinner and went back to my place and got to sleep. I didn't tell Sir yet that I was leaving for sure, but I had told him several times over the past few weeks that I was thinking about it. He refused to hear it and kept suggesting we find a place together instead. Thursday morning, I called a moving company. I didn't know what to say, so I literally said, "Hello. This is odd. I have a bunch of stuff in my apartment but I'm moving across the country and not taking it, so can you just come get it, and throw it in the trash downstairs? How much will that cost?"

The mover man informed me this was called "Labor Only," and for the amount of stuff I told him, he quoted me a good price. Done and done. The only problem was that T and I didn't leave until Saturday, and they were coming Friday (didn't want to wait until last minute!), so, I knew they would have to leave at least a mattress behind from the guest bed or something. Oh well, T and I had bigger fish to fry. We started putting everything from my kitchen cupboards into trash bags. Legitimately six hours and 46 trash bags later, we had successfully gotten rid of the majority of my items. Or so we thought.

In between trash runs, I came across the printer/scanner from our old office. T looked at me and glanced at my ex's golf set. "Should we?" she said, with my mischievous, deceased grandmother's look in her eye. "Should we what?" I wondered out loud, throwing everything in sight in a trash bag. She pointed to the printer. "Remember that scene from *Office Space* where they smash the crap out of the fax machine to gangster music?" Me, "Uh, duh." It's only one of my favorite movies ever. I finally got what she was saying. So, we took the printer down to the parking garage, and we beat the ever-living crap out of it. Some guys came down to go to their cars, and here we were, beating the shit out of a printer with expensive golf clubs, jamming to gangster music. To say they wasted no time running the opposite direction would be an understatement. We even made a video for your viewing pleasure. If you don't know what I am talking about, please search "Office Space Scanner Scene" online immediately.

My neighbor, D, who was always doing something fun, texted me that it was his actual birthday (even though we celebrated it the weekend before), and he was doing a dinner at Fig & Olive and ordering a limo to pick everyone up. We were welcome to join. I wanted to make sure my cousin had a good time while she was here on this interesting journey with me, so I texted back "YUP." Kwanza (my nickname for T, don't ask) and I got dolled up and met everyone downstairs in the limo. There was a whole crew of us in there, including most of my ex's friends and my old couple friends. D asked how our day was. T said, and I quote, "Well, let's see. We threw out about 46 bags of trash. Except they weren't trash. They were all of Danielle's personal belongings." I realized how sad that was, but I just found the humor in it and laughed. I knew we were in for a fun one.

When T had first arrived, she told me about a man named DJ from another state who she was somewhat into. They kind of hit it off, but he had some baggage that made it tricky. Anyhow, T never liked anyone, so I found this intriguing. It just so happened that they were friends on Facebook, and DJ had checked into Orange County that night—I guess he was visiting randomly on business. She contacted him while we were heading out and invited him to meet up with us. He happened to be eating literally three restaurants over from Fig & Olive. T wasn't working at the time, because she just moved and hadn't started her new job, so I told her I would cover dinner and everything for our trip back.

Everything usually works out in the end, right? I was just happy to have her there.

We ordered some sort of fish, and I don't even usually like cooked fish, but it was delightful. I was just trying all sorts of new stuff these days. I went to the restroom, and Hesh showed up (the friend whose birthday we were celebrating when I met Sir at the nightclub). D ordered a bottle of vodka with dinner, so the drinks were flowing and the music was going. Being that T and I had only had a smoothie and some white fish, we were getting turned up to burn up. We would have made smarter choices, but we were living the gypsy lifestyle that day. At the end, the bill came, and D paid for all of it. On his birthday. I wanted to cry.

DJ showed up after we finished dinner, and T and I were in the bathroom. He made himself at home and chatted with the dudes, which I found super cool. A lot of times bringing a man into a group of several dudes was hard for them. DJ seemed to be reserved yet still held his own. Everyone headed for their cars, but the limo had broken down somehow, so we ordered Ubers. T decided to ride with DJ, Hesh offered me a ride, and the rest of the crew piled in an Uber SUV. I threatened DJ to take care of my girl and gave him the address for Mesa, our next destination where we were supposed to meet a group of D's friends who I ran into frequently and found hysterical.

Before our ride, Hesh said to me on the way out, "You are such a nice girl. I didn't remember meeting you the first time, and I remember your ex coming to Paul's once for like 20 minutes and bringing chips and beer and randomly leaving." I remembered that day because we were fighting and I think he left because I threatened to pack up my shit and bounce. Moving on. "I heard about what happened to you, and it sucks and you are still such a nice girl. That's really cool. I just wanted you to know that." Hesh had an odd way of being super sincere at the most random times. He was harmless, like he wanted to explore as many options as possible but he wasn't the type to hit on someone randomly.

In the car ride, I remembered that he was recently divorced, and I asked him what happened. It's only fair, since everyone seemed to know my story already. Word traveled fast around these parts. He was usually a pretty deep dude, but his answer was, and I quote, "She was really jealous. Every time I saw a girl I knew, and I know a lot of people, she'd say, 'Did you fuck her?' She always thought I was cheating on her. Then she stopped putting in effort. Like stopped dressing up, stopped doing her makeup. It just wasn't working."

I just replied, "Oh, well, alright," as we pulled into Mesa.

Shit got crazy from here. T and DJ got lost but finally made it. Everyone ended up on the dance floor. I'm not sure what ensued next, but DJ left at some point, because he had a flight the next day. There was a man I had met before named Allen, he lived in my community close to my building and was friends with Hesh and D. He hit on me once, and even though I wasn't really into it, D warned me to watch out for him. I took this seriously, because dudes know each other and I know he really did care about my safety at the end of the day, if nothing else.

Hesh and Allen told T and me that we were all going to an after party at D's, which was fine with me, because I lived in the same building. They offered to drive us, since the limo was broken, and I said, "Sure! Let's roll." We ended up at Allen's house for some reason, and he made us tiptoe into the townhouse because he had a pregnant roommate. Allen had his mattress on the floor with an adjoining bathroom upstairs. Hesh and I were sitting on the floor, joking and laughing. Allen kept commandeering my cousin into another room with him, and I kept getting up and pounding on the door to check on her. "Are you okay?" T kept opening the door and assuring me she was fine. I went back and talked to Hesh, when I remembered what D had said about Allen. I kept yelling, "Kwanza! Are you ok?"

Hesh kept laughing. "Dude, she said she is fine."

Kwanza: "Yes I am fine!"

Hesh: "She says she's fine!"

Me: "Kwanza, are you fine?"

Allen: "Be quiet! My roommate is pregnant!"

I guess I was over-protective. It then dawned on me in a moment of semi-sobriety—why the hell were we at this man's house? I literally lived right next door. I commandeered the party and made everyone come to my place where we could play music and be loud without waking preggy. My apartment was scraps of what it used to be, with just two couches and some random paraphernalia. And I didn't have much booze left except a case of VOCO (vodka coconut water) that had been given to my ex to try out for his restaurant in Beverly Hills. So, I handed those out and put on some jams.

What ensued next was pure brilliance. T and I decided to start a bonfire on my balcony using my engagement album and wedding books, but I realized I had thrown out all my fire-starting items. I tried to just set it ablaze on my stove burner, and when that didn't work, T lit a paper towel, tossed the flaming piece of paper into a trash can with the wedding book, and hurried the trash can out onto the balcony. With my remaining bottle of 100 proof peppermint schnapps, the fire went from zero to hero—three-feet tall flames with smoke everywhere. The two guys started freaking about the fire like some paranoid pussies, and T shouted, "Shut up! We are from Wyoming! We know fire!" We stood and nostalgically watched the remainder of my memories burn until the sun came up.

Part 3:
The Climb

.

Chapter 19:
Two Years Later

I don't think anyone can truly explain tragedy until having lived through it. It's difficult to describe my situation, since it happened so suddenly, but when we got divorced, it truly felt like a death (except that my ex is still alive and constantly badgering me). People will tell you that marriage is life-changing. I could not disagree more. Divorce is life-changing. Death is life-changing. Cancer is life-changing. Marriage is a decision that two people make of their own accord, or at least that's what it's supposed to be. It's a natural progression in a relationship and a major milestone, but it doesn't completely alter your life overnight in the way a death, divorce, or diagnosis does. Even though I went through a lot with my marriage, I do still believe in marriage personally, and for those who decide to walk that path, I hear it can be a truly beautiful thing. I guess I don't know if I necessarily got to have the normal marriage experience. I'm not even sure I got to have the "normal" divorce experience (if there is one). There wasn't an unwinding period of our relationship. He basically pled guilty to a felony, came home, tried to cheat on me (I couldn't figure out why at the time) because he knew he was going to jail, flew to his court date, and never came home. However, divorce will change your life. Marriage just makes a life progression more permanent. Plus, divorce has such an icky connotation to it. Tell someone you just got married and you can almost see the bliss radiate out of their pores "OH, wow!"

Say you just got divorced and there's this awkward pause followed by uncomfortable banter.

Reflecting on the ways that my life has changed as a result of my marriage, divorce, and everything that followed would really be impossible, but I will say that with a different perspective, now that I have put some time and distance between the final situation and myself, I will never be the same person. At first, I was in a form of shock, and that shock later turned into a deep-seated depression. I am not a depressed person, nor have I ever really been. Yet, when something like that happens—I guess you could call it "a moment of tragedy"—it's almost like a poison boiling over in your center. You try your best to contain it, to channel it, to go through it, even to pour it out, but it just keeps bubbling over until it has affected every cell inside your being. The only thing that can rid you of it is time, healing, patience, and understanding (and for some, medication and therapy).

I remember in the darkest times after this happened, just sitting with this intensely horrific feeling in my body and wanting it to stop. I wanted it to go away. It was the opposite of what I think is natural for a human being to feel and everything about it was wrong. I kept asking my mom when I would feel normal again. I would Google on the Internet to see how others got through such a tragic state. I read books about other people's tragedies and Googled asinine things that I prayed would give me some sliver of hope of when this would end.

I know, now, that it never ends. Not really. Time has made it easier, and I was able to become stronger, to refocus and rebuild. But just like the Twin Towers that were so grotesquely torn down, a new and glorious tower now stands in its place. Below that tower, though, are the shards of the old buildings left in the soil upon which the new foundation was built, and that is how I mostly feel. I have come a long way and things have transformed and changed. I have overcome many things and have gained strength in unimaginable areas, but that situation and the wounds it caused are there underneath somewhere. I have just built on top of what remains of my tragedy within me, a new foundation, new walls, a new building. I wish someone would have told me in that moment, though, that it never goes away. Not really. Not completely.

I wish someone would have come to my house and literally moved in with me and watched me like a toddler during this time. It would've pissed me off, and I would have hated it, but even the simplest of tasks, initially, and for quite a while, really were unbearable. Checking the mail was like running a marathon. Paying a bill may as well have been constructing the great wall of China single-handedly, because it took every ounce of my being most days not to completely sink into nothingness, and, by God, I wanted to just sink. If I hadn't been living states away from my family, I would've just gone to my parents, gotten in bed, closed the blinds, and not emerged for several years. I'm not kidding.

For some reason, I just didn't have that choice inside of me and I couldn't let go of my dreams. That girl who fought so hard to live on her own terms wasn't giving up that easily. He wasn't going to win. After all the shitty relationships I'd been in, the friends who'd tried to bring me down, the situations I'd endured, the deaths around me, I was still standing. And the one bastard who truly cut me to the core and brought me to my knees, almost breaking me, breaking my spirit, the very essence of me as a human being, I had willingly invited into my life in every way imaginable. I spent years of my life with this person, getting to know him on what I thought were the deepest levels, sharing my hopes and dreams with him. I had worked so hard to be vulnerable with him. I had overcome everything else. And my own husband is the one who almost obliterated me. Ain't that some shit.

If I'd had a babysitter during this initial tragedy to come wake me up every morning, who would've made me go to some soul-filling place like yoga or church or an ashram or friggin' Soul Cycle, who would've fed me healing foods like fruits and vegetables and made me shower and rest. If this babysitter would have then forced me to meditate in a corner for 10 minutes, even though I would've found it grueling and a waste and awful, and then forced me to get out in the sun around positive and regular people, well, that babysitter would've really been the only alternative to perhaps a more positive spin on this whole healing process I've gone through. Instead, I pretty much had my damn self to rely on. No offense to my fabulous family, who called me and cared and hurt with me and cried with me and was there for me. I just mean that the everyday motions were up to me to figure out.

It was really up to me, to keep me out of the depths of hell, and I may have done a pretty shitty job of it, but I did do the best I could. I worked too much, slept too little (let's be real, if I slept at all, it was a miracle—you try shutting off your mind from this wacky bullshit), drank too often, ate too little, and mostly went through the motions with more awareness than is healthy. I dated, trying to squeeze some fun out of it. I went out there without expectation and only wanted adventure and guidance, and that goddamn torturous pain inside me to stop. I did unhealthy things and spent time around some really shitty people, and I just really couldn't see up from down. I was a broken woman. A shell of a person. A hole where a human had been. But I made it.

Dating a ton of different people had really shown me only one thing: dating is hard. Not in the sense of like "oh my gosh I feel so embarrassed what if he doesn't like me" hard, but like hard as in most people date really with an agenda in mind. As fun as it was, it also helped me to see into parts of these people's lives that I didn't want to become. I didn't want to become desperate and alone at a later age, having dated and partied myself out, when suddenly the lights of the club come on and I realize it's 2 AM, I'm too old to be here, and my chances at many things are rapidly expiring.

I didn't want to be the lonely workaholic who only cared about making a living and just longed to spend it with someone. I didn't want to be the wounded person who thought they didn't deserve a second chance. I didn't want to become that person who thought just anyone would do because, well, it's time to settle down. I was none of these people, and I wanted none of them in my life. I avoided the internal work I needed to do with every ounce of my being for as long I could. I dated a ton, drank too much wine, and when that didn't work out, I got busy. This worked well to avoid the pain, so I got busier and busier and busier. I could tell that life wasn't quite what it was supposed to be anymore, and, I hate to say it, but I couldn't even feel my emotions enough to heal them. It was seriously too painful.

People talk about repressed memories or blocking things out, and while I didn't necessarily experience that, I will say that I had a hard time feeling anything, in regards to that situation, for a very long time. People would bring up the subject of my divorce, and I would feel nothing. I knew I should have been extremely scared by my reaction, but there was no way to bring it up or down or around, or to access it at all. It was like grasping at dust outside on a windy day; I could sense it floating around, but I couldn't really capture it. I knew the emotions lived in my body, and I had seen the destruction that they had caused to my life and me as a person. I was not the same. I didn't know what to do next.

My time at home was nice but horrible at the same time. Normally, visiting home was fun because I had a life to return to ASAP. During my "sabbatical," that wasn't so much the case at all. I wanted to take the time so that I wasn't making decisions about my future for the wrong reasons, but it was hard being home. Everyone had their lives going on. I had zip to do. That could be fun in a place where there were lots of activities or say, a beach to go to, but there wasn't. Plus, it was October and that's when the weather starts going from cold to worse. I spent my days doing some exercise and sitting in the unsettling silence that my parents' land outside of town had to offer. It was probably needed, but it was also torture. At least I got to see my family and spend time with my parents, and both of my sisters, for the first time in a long time.

Halfway through my stay, after about two weeks, I flew back to California for a night for some meetings and to see Sir. We had so much fun together. As I sat facing the harbor with him having a cocktail, it was the first time I had relaxed in some time. He planned everything for my stay, got us a nice hotel room, took me to my favorite restaurant, and it made me wish that my time there wasn't coming to an end.

When I got back to Wyoming, family members made comments about things I could do there for work soon, houses I could settle into, you name it. It bothered me. It was never my intention to stay permanently. I know everyone was doing their best to give me options, to be welcoming, but it was still hard. After 30 total days, and a night out to see all the people I went to high school with, I looked around a bar that used to be so much fun for me to be at when I was younger. Suddenly, I realized it hadn't changed one bit. It would always be there. I would not be the same. I was not the same. I had more to do in the world. I needed to get out of this state of fog and grab life by the horns, to start living again, my way.

After almost a month in Wyoming, I called Sir, said I would be in California the next day, and accepted his invitation to live together. He called me often during my time home, had gotten a new place, and was awaiting my arrival. The fact that he actually seemed to want me there, instead of me just being a convenience, was nice. So, we'd split the bills and see how it went. His son also lived with him 50 percent of the time, so that was another large decision I had to make. It's hard to break up with someone when you live together, but it's even more unfair to drag a child through that. As a kid who grew up with divorced parents and stepparents, I was aware that this was a hefty situation to take on. I would forever have to deal with the ramifications if the relationship didn't work out, and would be the well-meaning enemy. And if things did work, there would be times when the kid would resent me for no reason except that I was not his parent. I would have to deal with Sir's ex for the foreseeable future, and I had no clue yet what kind of person she was or what that would look like. So, it was a *lot* to think about.

I left Frankie, my precious pug, in Laramie. My sister's two kids had fallen in love with him, and I wanted to get settled back in California before I dragged him across the country again through chaos. I also didn't know what kind of work I would be returning to, so it would be difficult. I was prepared to work five jobs at once if needed, and didn't want to leave the poor guy alone by himself all the time. I took a bit more time off work when I first got back to really just focus on things like sleep, exercise, and having fun. In the back of my mind, I was terrified about what the hell I was going to do with myself, but I had to keep moving forward and just knew that I would find a way. I was back where I belonged and that gave me the willpower to move forward. I was also surrounded by people who cared about me, like actually cared about me and my health and well-being, for a change.

I worked as much as I could in real estate, before life had its way of pushing me in new directions after being royally screwed over by some "friends" I worked with—and, yes, there were times they had done a lot for me, which I am still thankful for. But during my sabbatical, a house I co-listed with Paula closed. She wrote me out of the deal illegally and kept my commission money. I spoke with real estate attorneys and my family, and I had her dead to rights to press charges. Apparently, Paula claimed she did it because she thought I had stolen a lead from her for a house leasing some months earlier.

I heard all of this through a third party, and if she had brought it up to me, I would have walked away from that $600 commission check, no problem. I had already lost everything. But it was legally my deal. So, a few months later, she decided to have a client write me off a deal, because I was not in the area at the time and no one informed me it was closing. I was there the first time the buyer toured the property with an agent. I was that agent. I was also there to do the initial listing walk-through with the client. I deserved my commission, because the only other person there was Paula, who was not a licensed agent.

Because of a $600 commission, she felt slighted, so she decided later to cheat me out of thousands by leaving me out of deals that I had been involved in. She proceeded to take that money to the bank and then buy a Rolex from my jeweler I introduced her to. I decided from here that, because of all I had already been through with shitty people, I should just let it go. If they needed the money so badly that they could justify double-crossing their friend, they could keep it. I didn't have the space to hold on to that negative energy any longer.

I also knew that if I took Paula to mediation, her partner would lose the brokerage license and Paula could never get her license, which was an important goal for her. I didn't want to work for, with, or near this kind of thing anymore, but I couldn't take away their ability to provide for themselves. All I had really wanted to build since I had left the hair industry was my own online business. After reading *The 4 Hour Work Week*, I was blown away by the possibilities of entrepreneurship. I wasn't expecting to work an hour a week, make a million, and spend most of my time on a beach somewhere overnight. I just wanted my hard work to lead me to a life designed to fit my hopes for the future. H wouldn't ever listen to me about where the world was going and how a virtual business that you can do from anywhere was really where it was at. He started to towards the end, by getting involved with Network Marketing opportunities, but he never really heard me or cared to listen. His loss.

I had been pestering my best girlfriend who rented my other room, Ari, about working together for a few years, and, one day (after we had both moved out obviously) she called me. She knew I was debating what to do next with my life and was really in need of some direction. I had done work for some people she had referred me to in the online space years earlier, and it had been a great experience. She knew of some online entrepreneurs that needed major help with the small tasks while launching their businesses. I also had a certain skill set and background that she thought I could leverage in this field.

I said, "Fuck, yes, I'll do it." I didn't know what else to do at the time and frankly, I just saw an opportunity and dove into it head first. All the little, bitch work tasks most people who had held my many positions would have scoffed at? I did them with a smile. I didn't care how little or how big they were, I was just happy to be back working with positive people in creative spaces, with freedom to make my own life again. I was actually in control of when I ate lunch, when I wanted to start my day, and how. It was fucking beautiful. Now, don't get me wrong, some of the work sucked sometimes and it was hard friggin' work at that, but I just kept doing it, kept showing up.

I started working for myself, with help and advice from Ari, I started a decent business working for other entrepreneurs online. This seemed to be my best bet after being so royally screwed over (though I no longer blame Paula, which I will explain more later on). I threw myself into my work with reckless abandon. It consumed every moment of my day and, as I got busier and busier and busier, I realized that I was still wildly unhappy. It seems work had taken the place of all the other distractions I had made for myself previously.

One day, I was finally going through bank and credit statements and all that adult bullshit that people have to do. Taking time off to go home and not work and giving myself a bit of space when I came back to Laramie, along with my bills, had left me in a pretty precarious situation. The huge charges on my credit card, along with all the bills I was forced to pay for alone, all thanks to my ex-husband, were really ruining my credit. I needed to do something. I wasn't making the kind of money I was used to, and even though I was heading in the right direction, I just needed to figure something out financially in the meantime. I could've made it scraping by the next year or so with what I had going, but it was doing serious damage to my credit score with my debt-to-income ratio, and I knew I needed to make a big girl decision. I had already gotten rid of almost every fabulous thing I owned and there was really only one thing left worth anything that I had and could sell. My car.

Now, if you live in California or a city that is spread out, you know it's pretty much impossible to survive without a car. Yet, with the invention of Uber, it was possible to do so for a while, and all I needed was a while. I looked up the value of my car to get an idea of what we were looking at. I had purchased it from a car dealer in LA who was, surprise surprise, very good friends with my ex. He had given me a decent deal on it and the car was paid for, so I was hoping to get enough money from it to pay down the credit card debt.

Turned out when the car dealer my ex had been such good friends with had provided me with a Carfax report and signed paperwork stating it had a clean record on the car, it was total bullshit. The car had been wrecked before I bought it, and, even though it ran great, everyone was offering thousands less than I was expecting. Thousands. Now, I could've cried or cursed the sky above or had a *Steel Magnolias* meltdown, but I had already been to hell and back, remember? This was a cakewalk in comparison. I wasn't even surprised at this point. Anyone he had ever so much as bought a sandwich from on a regular basis seemed to have a special brand of fuckery up their sleeve.

I consulted my parents and Sir, and after everyone thought I was making a good decision in selling it, I still was going back and forth with what to do. It was my baby. I had worked hard for this car. It was all I had left. I got in it one day to drive to the store and my check engine light turned on. The car was a Mercedes that had just crossed 60,000 miles and was no longer under warranty, and the check engine light just decides to come on? I took it as a sign. The car had to go. The next day I drove it with Sir, and the check engine light had turned back off. I sold it that day before anything else could go wrong.

I paid down a few thousand dollars of the credit card debt, enough to make my credit score healthy again, and didn't look back. So, what was it like not having a car in a California while also working from home and needing to be an adult and get shit done? Or, heaven forbid, you want to go somewhere and do something fun? Well, it sucked ass. You feel like a kid who has to wait for the real adults to have time to take you places. It sucks for the people around you, too, because instead of being able to help them out with menial tasks, you have to do them on a schedule. They have to take you, or have to stay home so you can borrow their car. Unless you can just Uber, and that isn't conducive to, say, grocery shopping.

One day, I said, screw it! Car gods, you will not stop me from grocery shopping on my own damn terms! Shaking my fists at the sky, I walked to the grocery store. I bought groceries. And I walked my happy ass home with my groceries, in my grocery cart, that I had stolen from the grocery store so that I didn't have to carry multiple bags all the way back home. Yes, I looked like a hobo. And once I had gotten home, I realized this really wasn't convenient, probably wasn't very smart, and definitely didn't make it any easier.

So yes, not having a car sucked. You know what sucks more? Letting stupid decisions you allowed to happen-with some asshole who tried to ruin your entire life because he is a selfish douche— also ruin your financial future and any options to own a home, buy a new car, or have the financial freedom to make decisions because you want to, and not because you have to hold yourself back. Again, temporary, short-term suckiness for hopefully a long term positive outcome.

As you can tell from all of this chaos, with a life in shambles, I dusted myself off and picked myself up somehow. The truth is, the important work was really done from within. Something within me was unfulfilled and was hungry like a lion, roaring in the background. I tried to muffle it. I would look at myself in the mirror and not only did I not recognize the person looking back at me, I felt as if I wasn't inside of my physical body at all. It was if I was standing next to myself. And, to be honest, it scared the shit out of me. But what do you do in this situation? I tried to work on myself as much as possible. I read every book I could get my hands on about how and what to do to make yourself and your life better, from laws of attraction, to success, to journaling; you name it, I read it.

I finally stumbled upon two fateful opportunities that started to nudge me in the right direction. A girlfriend of mine tagged me in a post in a Facebook group we were both in about a woman named Frances who was giving away 100 free personal coaching spots. All you had to do was put your name down. "Screw it," I thought as I typed my name and hit enter. Whatever it is, I am game to try it. I scheduled my coaching session for later the next week and called her from the balcony of the building near my house. As I sat outside and discussed with her the situation and where I found myself now, what I was struggling with, she asked me point blank, "What is it you feel your purpose is in life?"

I tried to explain to her that ever since this situation had happened, I felt this pull deep within my soul to help women. I wanted to help women stand in their strengths, to understand that they could be, do, and have anything that they wanted and desired in their lives. That their life could literally be by their own design and that they were capable of anything. The societal norms and the regulations people put on us from the outside, or only by our own admission, weren't real. I wanted moms to know that they could travel and have the businesses that they wanted, that single women were allowed to feel worthy, that every woman should own her own piece of the world, and to stop letting others put us in a corner and influence us into taking a back seat. We may be great backseat drivers, but ultimately this is not where we belong. I had always known I was worth something and was supposed to do something of great importance with my life, and I felt a true calling from outside and from within; I just had no idea how to actually do it.

She said, "I believe in soul contracts. I believe that each of us signs one when we come to this earth. Perhaps your ex's soul contract was to make sure that you step into your power to impact and change hundreds of thousands of women's lives. Sure, it sucks, and I can certainly understand being mad at him, but his soul contract required him to be in these very unpleasant situations to catapult you into who you could be. He had to go to prison. You get to change lives. At the end of the day, you win. He was only a conduit to your betterment."

I was still pissed off at him and the situation, and it sickens me to my very core, his ability to deceive me and to leave me in the state that he did, to think of all of the people he hurt and the lives he destroyed. I was only one of the people in his long, hurricane path of destruction. Yet, looking at this from her standpoint actually made sense. Had none of this ever happened, I don't think that I ever would have had to become this person. I lived out loud and passionately before and did things on my own terms, but was very much roped into building things at the time for my spouse. He didn't allow my full light to shine the way that it needed to. He was threatened by my power. Now I had nothing to hold me back, and I would have to become the person I needed to be, to do the work I was called here to do. Sure, it may sound insane, but it's the honest truth. Shit be cray up in here.

And then I had another call that impacted my life. A prospective client wanted to hire me to help her launch her program, get her tech set up, and help to manage such an undertaking. She explained that she was a certified High Performance coach, which I didn't know much about at the time, but basically it meant that she was part of an exclusive program with Brendan Burchard on techniques to stay in high performance. I guess only a relatively small amount people in the entire world are certified as High Performance coaches, and she wanted us to get on a call as if I was a client, so that I could understand her business and what the people in her future course would go through.

She asked me a series of questions about my day, what my work was like, what my life was like. I knew I had shitty boundaries and was a "yes" person. I did not used to be this way whatsoever. I was almost ruthless before about standing up for myself and saying what I wanted and needed in almost any moment. Something about the shit box I received through that situation had really diminished that for me. I didn't trust myself or my judgment, and when you come from that place, it's hard to enforce pretty much anything concerning yourself. I was basically a skeleton who made it through the day with my emotions living in a box somewhere. I had become a workhorse with little more than tasks to be completed each day, from the moment I woke up until the moment I went to bed, and this included my personal relationships. It was as if everyone wanted what I could offer to them. After hearing about my usual daily life and my relationships, she said, "It sounds to me as if you give a whole lot of yourself. If you give and give and give and do and give and do, who is it that gives and does for you? What fills you up?"

I couldn't answer her. That sounds horrible, but I really couldn't think of anyone on a regular basis who regularly did much of anything for me. That's not to say that I don't have some amazing friends and family, who have gone out of their way to do whatever they could, but on a consistent basis in the way that she meant, I couldn't think of a single person. "You know," she continued after many moments of me not saying anything, "you are not an ATM. You can't just put out unlimited resources all the time without replenishing yourself somehow. You need someone to make deposits. They can't all be withdrawals."

Well, holy shit. You know the country song (I am not a huge country fan but it's fitting for my extended sob story) "Why Didn't I Think of That?" Really, I had never thought of that. With all of this newfound information, I had an idea of what I wanted to do, where I was headed, and how I wanted my life to look. This was all well and good. You can read six million self-help books and do the meditations and the journals and burn enough sage to asphyxiate yourself, and somehow still not know how the hell to actually do the things. I knew what I wanted to do and be; how to actually get there was the friggin' problem. So, I just kept putting one foot in front of the other.

Chapter 20:
Opening the Flood Gates at My Best Friend's Fucked Up Wedding

*R*emember earlier when I mentioned I had a hard time accessing my emotions? All of that changed at quite possibly the most inopportune moment ever. I guess we will have to start with the bachelorette trip for a friend from high school, who had asked me to be a bridesmaid in her wedding. I really debated writing about this at all, to be honest, because the events are embarrassing to talk about now, but this wedding was a catalyst moment that I have to include to tell my full story, against my better judgment.

Full disclosure, I am not saying she is bad or wrong, and I am not in any way diminishing her as a person, but we had been on different paths since high school graduation. Sometimes, you just don't end up being forever friends, and that's okay. This individual had said some really horrible things about me over the years, and as time went on it became more apparent that she just wasn't there to support and love me as a human. One of the greatest things I had learned about being an adult, is that we are allowed to decide who is in our innermost circle and who needs to be moved into the outer rings. She was someone I had moved into some outer rings some time ago. We lived in different states and had completely different lives. Although we stayed mildly in touch, we weren't close and hadn't been close for over a decade.

When she asked me to be a bridesmaid in her upcoming wedding, I was truly surprised, but I agreed because we had so much history together, and I felt that it was the right thing to do. For her bachelorette party, we were all to meet in Vegas and share a large suite. Sir ended up traveling there around the same time for some work stuff, so I thought it would be okay to go. I could hang with the girls, get some time with him, and then head back. Of course, I planned to stay in his room; I had long outgrown the sleeping-in-a-bed-with-three-other-people thing, without my own space and privacy after a night out on the town in Vegas. I could tell they were slightly annoyed that he was there, but they invited him out with us the first night when I introduced him. I didn't expect him to go, but they asked and he said sure.

I had gone to school with a lot of people in the group, but I hadn't lived in the small town I grew up in for over 10 years and our lives were worlds apart. I had a hard time really understanding them and their mindsets. They lived in small towns where you go directly to college, get a degree, get a 9 to 5 job and a 401k, and the dentist is the richest person you know. You snag a boyfriend and get married and then go on to work 40 years with vacations when you're allowed. We were just different people, nothing more and nothing less, but it could be awkward at times. I was very much an outsider in this situation.

The rest of the trip, the girls went out to clubs and pool parties, and I went along with them but they spent most of the time not as a group of girls, but chatting with strangers and doing this and that. I found myself alone a lot of the time, so I'd go off to hang out with my boyfriend because it's not as if they were going to notice. This wasn't a girl's kumbaya spa day, since they were all kind of doing their own thing, talking to guys, and scampering around here and there. Plus, I'm a grown-ass woman who paid to be there, so I didn't feel bad doing what I wanted to do. I worked constantly, and with the little time I was taking off, I was determined to enjoy it.

On the second to last day, Sir and I went to a pool party with the girls, and I had a bunch of their chewing tobacco in my purse. It kept getting confiscated, so we started sneaking it in under our bikini tops. We got to the security bag check, and, I must admit that for the last 10 years or so, I have been a major psycho when it comes to nutrition and supplements. I love them. I am interested in them. And being that it had been a bit of time for me since I had been to the Vegas party all night world, I was not about to be drinking a whole lot without some major B12 and vitamin rejuvenation.

At the security line, the man was questioning some things in my purse. I know how suspicious it looked, and I don't blame them for wanting to look into it further. B12 powder mix just doesn't look good spilled all over your purse, especially in Vegas. As they took me away from my group of friends to investigate, the girls all headed inside. After they realized that all I had was a harmless instant mix for electrolytes, they let me go back to the entrance line, but at this point, the line was wrapped around the block. I really didn't even want to go watch them talk to a bunch of strangers all day, and didn't know why I was wasting my time here. I called the bride-to-be and said that the line was crazy and I wasn't sure they'd let me back in. She said, "Do you mind going and hanging out with your boyfriend because we are having fun and I don't want to leave?"

Uh, okay. Obviously, we weren't communicating well, but as it didn't sound like they gave a shit if I was there or not, I didn't really want to stand in that long line and deal with trying to find them, sober as a gopher while they were probably three shots deep by now at some random's cabana. Off the hook, I enjoyed the rest of our trip, went to the girls' dinner, and spent the rest of the time with my boyfriend. Upon leaving, the bride-to-be texted me asking me to pay my portion of the hotel room that I had been in for maybe an hour the whole weekend. I Venmoed the money and went back home to my life.

With the wedding approaching, I knew it would not be without some difficulty. I had been working 14 hour days with literally no days off since I had gotten back from Vegas. I was drained and exhausted in every sense of the word. This ATM machine was just giving wherever it could and not receiving much in return. The bride-to-be's sister would be styling hair for the wedding and asked if I wouldn't mind pitching in. There were five of us total, and I knew how much of an ordeal this can be, so I said I'd be happy to help (this was all prior to the bachelorette party of course). As I didn't even really know these people anymore and they certainly didn't know me, I thought at least I will have a function during the day besides sitting there awkwardly with nobody to talk to. Sir couldn't make it to the wedding with me, so I got to be the cool person who brought their mom as the date to the wedding (although she really is the most fun date ever, so I was excited anyway). It was just lightyears away from what my life looked like in the recent past as a married person with someone by my side, who (I thought) I could always rely upon to be there for me.

The day of the wedding, I showed up and helped with styling hair as we had planned, but feeling very sleep-deprived. We started having some drinks at an early hour, and between that and not having much to eat, it was really a disaster waiting to happen for me. But hey, everything happens for a reason. The ceremony was beautiful and the reception was gorgeously decorated, and even though there were some striking similarities to obvious choices I had made at my own wedding two years prior, I pushed that into the back of my mind and just tried to be present in this moment for her.

Some of the other bridesmaids basically accused one of our good friends of doing drugs at the wedding (even though he was sitting with my mom, you know, the sheriff). They tried to start some drama, but it just didn't work. I thought how ridiculous it was and avoided them the rest of the evening. It was a gorgeous event and just when the father-daughter dance came on with a slideshow showing the years of the couple together, so much flooded into my heart and mind about my own relationship, my own father, my own destroyed marriage and life, and, at the same time, overwhelming happiness for her in this moment. My heart was filled to the brim and with tears in my eyes, I said a silent prayer that she would never have to go through what I went through.

I kept running into people from high school, and, at this point, I was really on my last leg. Exhausted and having had too many shots bought for me by old friends, I was starting to crash hard. My stepdad came to pick my mom and me up, and my parents said, alright, I think it's time we get you out of here, which means I must have really started to cross into the hot mess zone. I loaded up into the car while my mom went to the "get ready" room (where the bride and all of us had prepared for the big day) and apparently got my suitcase that I had brought with all of my personal possessions in it, unbeknownst to me. We started to head home and suddenly, all of the hurt and pain and anger that I had not felt from my own situation broke free and hit me like rush hour traffic on the 405 freeway. I have never in my entire life cried so much or so hard or been so hysterical. I cried for myself and 32 other people at once. I could barely hear what I sounded like because my ears were so full of sadness, but what I could make out didn't sound human. It sounded like pure pain coming out of every orifice of my body. It broke out of me in every direction imaginable. I was an absolute wreck.

Now, I could blame it on the many, many drinks we had that day, the constant work and exhaustion, the old wounds of being in my hometown, around my parents and high school friends, or even being at a wedding, but the truth was that something had unleashed all the grief I had been completely unable to access for so long. And up it came. My parents had to practically carry me from the car to our house, and as tears spilled all over my bridesmaid dress, my mom helped me change into an oversized t-shirt. They made sure I was going to survive, and I cannot imagine what they were thinking (poor souls). I was a complete wreck.

Suddenly, my phone rang. It was the bride's sister, so I answered in case it was important. She had had her fair share of drinks too and started going off on me about how my mom had stolen her hair supplies. It made no sense to me. I was in the middle of an emotional and mental breakdown, and she is calling and saying my mom of all people stole her hair stuff? My mom doesn't even like to do her own hair, for Christ's sake. I said, "I have no idea what you are talking about," probably in much ruder terms than that, but it caught me off guard and I was not in a state to be approached about anything concerning my family that way.

My mom came in to check on me and I told her what had just happened, saying, "How weird is that for her to accuse you of stealing her stuff? Like WTF?" My mom pointed to a black suitcase in the corner that I had not seen before this moment. "Is that your suitcase?" She half grinned.

"Uh, no" I replied. "Oops," my mom said. Basically, my parents hadn't really seen much of the luggage I had brought home with me from the airport besides that it was dark colored and somewhat large. I guess my mom had tried to be nice and grab my bag for me (I thought I'd just get it the next day when we went to pick up her car), but had mistaken the bride's sister's bag for mine since it had a bunch of curling irons and things in it. It all made sense now, except the accusatory rudeness. My bag had all my clothes for my trip in it, everything that I had brought with me, jewelry, expensive shoes, and important paperwork for work that I needed. I wasn't calling them throwing a fit. I got a notification that her mom had reached out on Facebook to message me asking if they could get the suitcase back.

"No," I thought to myself, "I want to keep your hair kit and surrender all my personal belongings in return." What was the deal with these people? I was not happy to be treated this way. I messaged her back that all my belongings were still in the room and I obviously wanted those as well, so my mom would be happy to swap suitcases in the morning or drop it wherever, when she went to get her car at the venue. Not a big deal.

Then the bride texted me, "If you ever talk to my sister like that again, you and I are going to have problems. Also, my husband is mad that you were caught doing drugs at our wedding." I literally laughed out loud when I read that part. After all of these years and all of the times that she had put me down, belittled me, talked bad about my accomplishments or who I was as a person, this was really the last straw.

I realized in this moment that this was not the type of person I needed in my life anymore. I was feeling so much hurt and pain, that in comparison I realized they would never understand the depth of what true deception and destruction felt like. They would cling to the petty drama and nuances that they could muster up because of their lack of tragedy and compassion, and understanding about how much hurt and pain can happen in the world, and what is truly important.

I wasn't sure if she meant to actually accuse me of "doing drugs" at her bachelorette party and just said it wrong (which would at least make sense), or if she actually meant to accuse me of doing drugs at her wedding, but either way the fact that she knew so little about me that she could accuse me of any such thing, spoke all the volumes I needed to hear. There was no "thank you for traveling and being there for me and helping with hair and whatever was needed." Nothing. Just accusatory remarks. I said, "Don't ever fucking talk to me again." And that was that. I removed her from my life in this moment. I blocked her and those girls on her drug-sniffing panel from my phone and social media.

As I mentioned, I don't think this person is bad or rude or wrong or any of those things. There just comes a time when we realize who stands for our betterment, and clearly she and I just don't stand for that in each other. She works in some sort of drug counseling, so perhaps that's her go-to explanation, but I was done dealing with other people's problems. I was tired of the bullshit. And, you know what, after that, the strangest thing happened. Absolutely nothing.

I finished my cry fest and flew home the next day to return to work. It would be many more months before I sorted through all my bullshit, but I was happy that I could finally feel feelings, that I was human. I felt lighter somehow. I still had so much pain and destruction in my body from that event, but some of it had broken free in my whirlwind breakdown and gotten outside of me. Even though I surely scared my parents half to death, I think it took all of these moments and being in a safe environment, for it to actually bubble up and break free from where I had suppressed it all. Now, healing could finally start on some level.

Part 4:
The Top

Chapter 21:
A New Perspective

I used to base my worth off whether or not another human being found me to be cool, or deemed me worthy of their friendship or attraction. But I've realized that worth has nothing to do with these things. Every human being on this planet is born *valuable*. You have more value than you will ever know, because even if you could grasp a small percentage of how valuable you are, you would own the freakin' world and all of your dreams along with them. You are SO valuable that you cannot mentally comprehend it. This is why playing small and putting up with people, situations, and jobs that don't suit you are such a waste of time.

This revelation hit me recently. Sir and I had talked extensively about how I wanted my own family—not that I don't consider his son a part of that, but I wanted to be a mom. I looked around at my friends who had kids and the milestones they had been through, and looked back on my life. Sure, I've eaten at fancy restaurants in countries all over the world, partied at the best night nightclubs, VIP this and that, cool yadda yadda. I had never been sure that I wanted to be a parent, but I started feeling the pull toward eventually being a mom. Sir told me he would be honored for me to have his babies, which even though he already had one, was a sweet compliment.

After a tumultuous few weeks with him (being a step parent and sharing your partner with someone is hard and requires the other person to work on themselves A LOT), I went inward and asked for a sign about where I was supposed to go, big-picture-wise, in my life. I woke up in the morning feeling all over the place. The past week, I'd felt really up and down emotionally, which wasn't the norm for me. I was beyond exhausted. I took a shower and started gagging out of nowhere—not throwing up, just gagging.

Sir and I went to grab lunch across the street, and I felt so thirsty. He said, "I bet you anything you're pregnant." I wasn't sure but my body felt different than usual, so it was possible. We went to Target and bought a pregnancy test. I went home and took it, and as the two pink lines showed up, I looked at Sir to see how he would react. His response blew me away. With tears in his eyes, he hugged me and said, "You will be the best mom. The best mom. From here on out, whatever you need, you tell me, and I'll do it. It's not about me anymore." I was shaking. I was unsure if I was ready to be a mom. I was unsure that Sir could handle the juggling act of being a parent again. I was nervous about having a child with someone who had one already. All the new things parents experienced together for the first time would not be "new" to him. Would everything my baby did be compared to his past life by those around him? Would everything I did as a mother be compared to his past? I didn't care about that stuff, but I certainly didn't want to hear about it my whole life.

I am my own person, and I do things in relation to my beliefs. Pregnancy was a whole other journey that perhaps I'll write a book about another day. Especially as an unwed mother, I can't tell you how alone I felt at times. Going through the journey was not only isolating but difficult for me, because my partner had been there and done that already. There were these sweet, incredible moments, sure, but the best one was truly just having her. She blew my world into a pile of glitter and filled my life with love I had never truly known. She taught me what true and unconditional love is.

When my daughter, Vail, was born, I realized what it means to have value. Her only skills on this earth as a newborn were using the bathroom in a diaper, eating, and crying, yet she was and is still the most magnificent and valuable thing I have ever seen. Her very being radiates with the miracle that this life is. I think of some of the ways I have treated myself, or lowered my standards or settled or put up with things that didn't suit me, and I wonder why. I contemplate when I look at her why it took me so long to decide to become a mom. If my mom felt the wonders of me the way I feel the wonders of her, I can't imagine how hurtful it must have been for her to perceive me making choices that were so subpar. And, yet, at the time I thought it was all I could do, what I had to do, or "okay for now." I believe the Universe feels very much the same way.

Please. Stop. Allowing. Bullshit.

Life is beyond short. Be a badass motherfucker and ditch all the stuff in your life that doesn't make you beyond happy, and do it now. Don't be like me. I settled and stayed in a relationship far too long, clinging to the good times, and all it left me was betrayed, conned, and financially burdened with an open case of identity theft.

You want to talk about the law of attraction? I let this situation convince me that I was less than worthy, and it completely robbed me of my self-esteem. I remember thinking, "What must people think about me?" or "They probably think I am so dumb." I remember thinking people that have always judged and disliked me were probably celebrating and laughing at the fact that my wonderful life imploded around me. Now, through all of the hard work, learning, and coaching, I understand that our lives are a REFLECTION of what we believe to be true. Yep. Swallow that for a moment.

As soon as I started to believe all of those things, my life reflected them. I lost the nicest apartment I have ever lived in, I lost all of my money and was left with debt that wasn't even mine, I lost my luxury vehicle, I lost the great state of California as a home for a time, and, along with all of that, I lost my identity and self-worth. From there, I wondered why people were treating me so shitty, why they suddenly reacted differently toward me as if I were unimportant or worthless. I thought it was because I didn't have "all the fancy" stuff anymore. That is probably partially true (for some of them), but I now realize that it was actually because, number one, I put up with it (you get what you ALLOW), and number two, I believed these things to be true about myself, so my entire life reflected them back.

I am not saying that I deserved or created the chaos of a conman spouse. What I am saying is that, once in a while, when we don't listen to our true selves, when we allow things that we don't want to continue in our lives, and when destruction happens, we can sometimes make the situation we didn't deserve that much worse. I don't believe I created the horribleness of my ex's choices. Those are his seeds he sowed. I do believe that this situation was a catalyst for me to find my purpose in life for this chapter, to become who I needed to be in this moment, so that I could share this story and what I have learned, to hopefully help others in some way, shape, or form.

I also don't think I had to suffer quite so much with what I now know. I went, in a year and a half, from completely destroying my life and basically being homeless, living with my mom with no job, a bunch of debt, and a conman ex-husband with a jail sentence, to building a successful six-figure business, living in my dream location, finding my purpose in empowering women, and raising a beautiful daughter. But I would be so much further along if I'd had the tools that I do now PRIOR to this disaster happening. So, how in the hell do you dust yourself off after an explosion and rebuild your city (so-to-speak)?

Let's back up.

I built my current business out of complete and total need. I knew that would hopefully give me a small shred of something I didn't have in the rest of my life: control. My hope was to make my own schedule, to be my own boss, and to be able to make unlimited amounts of income, but that isn't exactly the way things started. When I first started my current business, it overtook my entire life. I worked with everyone out of fear. I never said no. I didn't know my time was valuable. I didn't know my gifts were valuable. I didn't know that I was valuable. It took me a long time—a year and a half of almost 80 hour weeks—to figure this shit out.

I built my business on a dream that I was more valuable and more intelligent than the offers available to me. I imagined the type of life I wanted to live, the type of person I wanted to be, and the bounds I wanted to live outside of. And I got started. In the beginning, a good friend hooked me up with some pretty stellar entrepreneurs. I was humble. I knew I wanted to be in that space and that I was meant to do huge things in this world, something a traditional job wasn't going to afford me personally. Yet, I started at the bottom (literally) and told my girlfriend who knew about the online world and knew my background, that I was willing to do literally anything for these people. This way, I could make money (more probably, than at a traditional, random job) and learn their businesses and tactics from the inside out.

If I didn't know exactly *what* it was I wanted to do, I would learn what I didn't want to do, and I'd learn it from people who were already doing it extremely successfully. I started reading, learning, taking courses, taking on jobs, anything and everything to get as much knowledge and as much experience as I possibly could. Sure, I had already run successful businesses before, but when someone has what you want, you swallow your sparkles and shit and listen to what they have to say. If they said do this, I did it. If they asked, "Hey, will you…" the answer was, "Yep." I didn't care what the task was, how little or how big. My friend taught me a lot. During my free time, I learned more. And more. And more. I had more knowledge at a certain point than I knew what to do with, and guess what? I was still just checking emails for some of these people. I didn't give a damn. I knew my time would come. I would learn the ropes and then I'd start swinging from them, MY way. I knew this was temporary.

At first, it paid my bills. Then it paid my bills and THEN some. Soon, I had to do what any CEO of their own business would do as my skills and offerings got to a certain point; I had to raise the bar for what I was willing to do and what I was willing to get paid for it. The first time I raised my prices, I was terrified. What if everyone said "no thanks" and hired someone else? I soon found out that not only was it still too little to ask for what I was worth, but also that there were very few people who did the job as well as I did. I also learned this the hard way, when I tried to hire internally for my own business. I was a hard motherfucker to replace.

Eventually I started handlinging digital strategy and tech for entrepreneurs and their launches, and I was good at it. It was like so many moments combined from my life gave me a certain set of tools that were made to do this sort of thing. Not just good, damn good. I was making more than I ever thought possible, and I was making other people obscene amounts of money (like, more money than people I grew up with spend on a *house*) in the just the span of a week, using the techniques I had spent a lifetime learning. I realized I needed to step out on my own in more ways than one. If I wanted to inspire other people to truly live their dreams and live life on their own terms, then I had to. If I believed it was possible for others to make unlimited amounts of money, then surely it had to be possible for me. It was time to start living it.

Chapter 22:
Making Money is GOOD

I remember there was a time when my thoughts and my feelings about money were SO fucked up. I'm not using that term for shock factor; I say it, because it was the truth. I went from busting my ass to make rent (and sometimes even asking my mom for help) to living a life that some people could only dream of. Then, my world came crashing down because of the choices and lifestyle of my ex. I took this as punishment for thinking that life could be so good, that I could live a certain way, that I deserved nice things, that I was valuable. There were lessons to be learned here, but my thoughts and relationship with money didn't need to be impacted so badly as a result. Yet, they were.

Being a proponent of self-help and working on my mindset early on helped me learn these lessons more quickly, and counter some of the negative lessons I had taken on from childhood and people around me. Believe it or not, my ex also had some positive effects on my mindset. For instance, he taught me that you can be anyone you want to be. He was surrounded by a lot of really successful people who had done amazing things, and they always had good advice, and optimistic outlooks. He taught me that it wasn't glutinous to be comfortable. He was huge into self-care and taking the time you needed to reharness your energy and concentration. He wasn't all work and no play. But he polluted all of the positive effects with his own toxic beliefs and his ability to lie, cheat, and steal. My mindset was something that I had actually worked on earlier in life as well, but I didn't truly absorb and understand fully, until life turned around and kicked the ever-loving shit out of me.

With my newfound business alongside these extremely successful entrepreneurs, the one thing they all had in common was their focus on underline_development and mindset. Why is this underlined? Cause it's freakin' important, yo. All of them invested in some sort of higher learning, read personal development things, and surrounded themselves with people who had higher personal and professional achievements than they did. And, sure, even though some of them had a chip on their shoulder, they were open to working on themselves to constantly and consistently become BETTER.

I asked them to reflect back to me the types of things I was doing and saying, that were not in alignment with what I wanted. For instance, when I was finally making money, I would buy myself something with the thought of "Oh, well, maybe I shouldn't buy this because later when I have nothing, I will be mad that I bought this because money will be tight and I'll think shit I wish I wouldn't have bought whatever the hell that was because then I'd have an extra $100 and that $100 may not be hard to come by now but it probably will be in the future."

Maybe you are laughing at me—laugh all you want—but I went from someone who had it all, to losing everything I had worked my whole life to gain. Flying in a private jet one week, living with my mom the next. If you resonate with that thought process, then you know how hard life can be and how your mindset can make or break a lot of this, especially when it comes to money.

When I stopped allowing myself to think that way and changed my perception, everything around me changed. I started thinking, "Yep, I spent that $100 on that thing, because it made me feel good and I deserve nice shit. I'm going to rock that $100 item, and I'm going to love the way that it makes me feel. And when I feel good, I naturally draw more good shit to me. And I make more money. Money is a renewable resource, and I'm renewing it right now." Sure, it sounds insane and maybe people at the mall thought I was off my pills or just a space cadet for being so in my head, but this was something I literally had to go through to change my relationship with money.

I think it became the most apparent to me where my money issues were, when I went to change my prices. I increased them a lot because I had waited too long and was way over-delivering, and way under-charging. When I started talking to other people in my industry, I realized the scale used for charging for things was not what I was using; I was basically the massage parlor giving out happy endings for half price. I needed to go from free hand job to high-class hooker, pronto. When I approached my clients with my price change, a few of them were like, "Uh, duh! Not a problem." One of them protested and it caused me to have a heart attack. Finally, the person relented and decided to pay what I had asked, but I still fell into the same trap of over-delivering, always making myself available and working twice as hard, because, you know, I had asked for a more livable wage for the amount of work I delivered, so I better bust my ass ten times harder. It was insane.

It wasn't until I really dug deep and worked extremely hard on my beliefs and changing them at the core of my being, that things started to shift. I still think I have a long way to go in this department, but when you start to learn about the ways people cheat themselves with their bad money mentality, you start to see it as a "tell." When you say, "I bought this thing BUT," that's a huge red flag. When you find yourself explaining away why you bought something, that's a sign you need to work on your own money mindset, not because I am telling you to, but because you deserve it. It will change your life for the better, and also turn you into a crazy person who is hyper-aware of the verbiage that others use when they talk about money (a little-known side effect).

So, what is money mindset and all this stuff anyway? It's just a buzz word term for basically your belief of whether or not you deserve something, and the actions and terms you use during, before, and after that happens. It's a reflection of what you believe to be true in the Universe, and it will greatly affect how you live, what you charge for your work, and what you can accomplish in this world. So, yes, it's pretty damn important.

Recently, a relative who will remain anonymous bought a boat. This person had been looking at boats their entire life. Now, they could afford a boat (or 2 or 3), but they nonetheless put off getting on for YEARS. They finally came to the decision to just go ahead and purchase one. They bought a real badass of a boat. I mean, the kind of boat you buy after dreaming of one for 50 some years. For real, it wasn't a yacht or some cruise ship, but as far as fishing boats go, it was basically as nice as you could get. This person said to me when I remarked how nice it was, "Yes, it is a really nice boat, but don't worry, we bought it used." My response? That is nobody's business if you bought it new or used or by giving blowjobs in South Beach. That is your friggin' boat. Don't explain it away. This person has worked their entire life, has taken care of people, and has never bought frivolous items for themselves so that they could provide the best available for their children, family, and friends.

YOU do not have to explain away your purchases. You are WORTH nice things. If you have a belief system that you are not, and you are explaining away your expensive purchases, you have some real work to do in your money relationship. The other thing people are guilty of is negative money talk. I HATE hearing the terms "I can't afford it" or "I'm poor" come out of people's mouths. You should not ever say these words. What you are really saying is, "I don't think I deserve it," "I don't think I am worthy of it," and "I don't believe it's possible for me." That is a horrendous thing to believe about yourself. If you say things like, "I never have enough money," it will continue to be true.

Don't tell yourself, "I can't afford it." That is a powerless statement. If you were so powerless, your God, your Universe, whatever you believe in would not have allowed you to exist. Sorry, but it's true. Try saying, "I am choosing not to spend my money on that at this time." If you have kids, this is extra important. Don't tell them "we can't afford it." Instead, tell them, "We aren't spending our money on that right now." Try it. See how much better it feels.

Now, that doesn't mean anytime you see something you want you should just pull out a credit card and charge your life away, because it will somehow "all work out." What I am saying is that we all can *choose* what we spend our money on. Sure, maybe that expensive purse doesn't make sense to buy when you need to pay rent. You can simply say, "I am choosing not to spend money on that at this time." When it makes more sense for you and you are a bit more comfortable with it, perhaps you will choose to just go ahead and buy the damn thing.

If you see something you want that is way outside of your budget, instead of repeating how far off it is, just tell yourself, "I deserve to have nice things like that, and everything I desire to have is mine." It just feels a lot better. Plus, it's actually TRUE. What you tell yourself shows you what your true beliefs are, conscious or unconscious. The sooner you do some healing on that shit, the sooner you will start to live in a better way. You are going to have to do the real work.

A big piece of striving for improvement and having a healthier relationship with money is learning to take care of yourself. This one is HUGE. Everything on our planet has an energy vibration. You need to be an energetic match for what you want and a ton of money has a higher vibration. Why? There is more of it. SO, why do we wear ourselves out and down working and slaving nonstop, lowering our own vibrations to get it? Everything in life is a reflection of ourselves, so if we have a super low and worn out vibration, our money state may reflect that. Sure, it's not always the case, but even if you are treating yourself like a slave and are making great money, you will eventually burn out. You will also get sick of teaching yourself that making money is "hard" and then really screw up your money mindset some more. You may actually start to repel it.

The point is, you need to work on raising your vibration. You can do that by taking one step each day to do something that brings you joy, happiness, relaxation, a smile, you name it. It can be extremely simple, or it can be extremely extravagant. It can take one minute, or it could take three hours. The choice is yours, but when you start to focus on yourself, you will be amazed how everything else in your life starts to flow without conflict. It becomes, as my mentor coined it, easy.

Life doesn't have to be a constant state of struggle and work. It should be fun and easy for you to make money. If it's not, you just have some changes to make. You do not live in the same world that your parents or grandparents grew up in. Hard work is important, but it doesn't always have to be hard. You have opportunities available to you that didn't even exist ten or even five years ago. Think about that for a moment. Sure, it may be difficult to shift these thought processes at first, but it gets easier. When I started really paying attention to the things I said, I started to notice my beliefs around them. When I did the work to change those beliefs, my life started to reflect that. When I started taking care of myself and raising my vibration, I made more money and I worked faster and with more ease.

For real, I even logged into my PayPal account one day to find a few extra hundred dollars from nowhere. I once received a Venmo for a thousand dollars for no reason. Clients offered me more. I received higher bonuses for the same amount of work. People gave me free stuff. It's incredible what can happen. Sure, it could all be a load of shit and just random coincidences, but everyone I know practicing these techniques has this result. So, what do you have to lose besides struggle and frustration?

And, let's be honest, a lot of that struggle and frustration probably stems from how you think about spirituality, religion, God, The U. For me, my spirituality has changed overall as I've embraced personal development. I don't believe in a punishment mindset and most of my life struggled to fit into a traditional religion. I have always felt that the world had this vibration and energy, and there was so much more to it than we could comprehend. I always believed in a higher power that orchestrates the universe and that everything happens for a reason. I don't think it's necessary to get into my specific beliefs, because everyone is different and I feel that respecting that is important.

However, it is important to realize that taking care of yourself is taking care of your creator, whoever you choose to recognize that as. Putting yourself first is putting the person who made the universe (and you) first. Buying yourself nice things doesn't piss that person off. Wouldn't your parents actually want you to have the best of everything? (And if your parents are assholes, then let me apologize for using that example and just say that, yes, your parents should want you to have the best of everything). The universe and God in all of its glory and expansiveness actually want you to be happy and have all the things you can imagine. It's just as easy for it to give you a tube of lip gloss as it is a million dollars. There is no difference to it, but it can only help you so far before your beliefs start sabotaging things.

I have realized that there isn't a "punishment" system. Sure, the universe or higher powers that be do generally favor those with a higher vibration, because LIKE attracts LIKE. Oil and water don't mix. Don't be oil and expect your world filled with water. You have to start acting and operating in a way, that the person you want to be at your very core would. Only then will you start to make real changes, and so will what shows up within your life. When I was able to let go of my ex's ideas of punishment and guilt, I was able to see more clearly the truth that I felt was out there all along, and to align more deeply with what makes sense for me. Listen to your heart and your intuition when it comes to your spirituality. It is inside you, not an external thing that you have to find. If you start listening to that quiet voice inside, the one that you know is there, you won't steer yourself wrong.

Chapter 23:

Women Are the Most Powerful Creatures on the Planet

I believe that women are the most powerful creatures on the planet. We create life in our bodies. Think about that. We literally have the ability to make life inside of us. Sure, not all by ourselves, but after that initial part, yes, we very much do the heavy lifting. And after we create it, we birth it, keep it alive, and nurture it, all while balancing 1,000 other things. This is incredible. We are strong, we are emotional, we are brilliant, and we are capable of more than we give ourselves credit for. I truly believe that women need to come together more and realize how brilliant we are. That we don't need to tear each other down out of fear that we aren't good enough, or won't have what what's her name has. We are unlimited and boundless beings that can do incredible things.

I want any woman where I was, to know that she is capable of anything that she wants. We were not created or put on this earth to just eat shit all the time and live on other people's terms. We are put here to create the life that we want and desire. Unfortunately, we don't get what we deserve; we get what we believe deep down on the inside *to be true.*

You must stop being so afraid to color outside the lines. Stop being afraid to take chances. Start listening to that voice inside of you that tells you what your real desires are and go for them. NOW. The only boundaries of what we can have and create are the ones that we put on ourselves. You know that girl you follow on social media, the one that travels all the time with unlimited amounts of money, wearing the best clothes who seems to have zero problems in life? First, she probably does have a shit load of problems (they just aren't as fun to post, imagine #cryingselfie—not so cute). Second, she probably pisses you off. She probably pisses you off, because you don't think that is possible for you. BUT IT IS. Your triggers all exist to show you what you are avoiding, or what you want to be more like. They are all telling you something. They aren't bothersome, random things that occur just to piss you off. They are KNOWLEDGE that you can use to make changes to yourself (and therefor change your reality).

Don't be afraid to try to go for your dreams and fail. My entire life, I wanted to be a published author and write a book. I could never figure out what to write about. Through one of the worst situations and my biggest failures to date, this book you are holding in your hands was born. On the other side of my biggest mistakes and lessons were some of my biggest dreams. When I prayed that night in the bathroom that God and the Universe would take from me that which no longer served me, I knew that changes would come. I let it go. Less than a month later, my ex was ripped from me and my old life burned down with it. Ask and you shall receive.

I never would have become all that I am or do the things that I wanted to do, if that situation stayed the same. I don't want you to go through the hell, and all of the pain or the suffering that I went through—I don't wish that upon anyone—but I want you to realize what you are worth. Wake up to the fact that you are worthy and capable of accomplishing your desires. Stop being afraid to go for your dreams and stop letting excuses get in the way. The only thing in your way is your own mind. Feed your mind goodness. If you need some other incredible books (besides this one of course) to help you on your journey, I have some of my favorites listed on my website at www.books.danielleprahl.com.

I have so many incredible women in my life that I see holding themselves back, because of what they believe or what society tells them to be true. I knew someone with a little baby who desperately didn't want to be with the father anymore, but felt that if she broke up with him that no one would want to date her because she has a baby. Are you telling me that there wasn't a man out there who would cherish the incredible fucking gifts of human beings she and her child are? That he wouldn't thank the lucky stars every night that they were both created? Because, there was a man out there who would feel that way. The only thing holding her back from the happiness that she knew in heart she deserved was HERSELF.

Sure, walking away from a relationship when you have a child is frightening. It's hard. It's not just you that you have to think about anymore. However, the relationship has served its purpose and, in this case, it has very much run its course. In her case, I believed everything she was waiting for was on the other side of it. And, no, I am not encouraging all women with kids to break up with their spouses. I am talking about a very specific scenario here. Obviously, when families stay together and can be happy, that is ideal. However, this was not the case here. And, guess what? This girl walked away from that relationship and did indeed meet the man of her dreams. It happened fast and it happened easily. What if she had never had the lady balls to do it? She'd probably still be sitting unhappily next to a man who didn't love her enough to work on their relationship and be the spouse she truly deserved, allowing her to be the woman she desperately knew she could be. She'd be teaching her child to settle, to be boxed in, to not go for their dreams. Instead, she gets to teach her child what a loving, happy, healthy relationship looks like every day. Good for her.

If you have wanted to be an author, a teacher, a lawyer, someone who travels for a living, I challenge you to start taking chances. Start taking actions every day toward that goal. You don't have to figure it all out or know exactly how it will happen. You just have to believe that it is possible. Believe in yourself and know that you are worthy of the desires inside of your heart. Your time is incredibly valuable. Stop wasting it on things that don't matter. There are women who make money posting about tea in their underwear on Instagram. There are men who make money playing their favorite sports. There are kids who make money showing off their toys on YouTube. ANYTHING is possible. The Internet has literally taken away the boundaries of space and time. It's no longer difficult to start a business or make connections with those who can assist you in upleveling your life. You have no excuse anymore. You have been given all the tools to become what you desire to be, do, and have.

People telling me I couldn't create a good life by myself infected my way of thinking, and it was a long time before I realized that they couldn't imagine it for themselves, therefore they couldn't imagine it for me. Sometimes, people want to keep you safely in the box that makes sense in their own minds, because they don't think they are capable of things, so why should you be? That would be truly uncomfortable for them. It would challenge everything they believe in and show them that they are missing out on their true potential, and that would be frightening for them. Maybe they are comfortable in their safe little bubble where challenging the status quo is scary.

I am not that person, and if you are holding this book in your hands, I don't think that you are either. Other people's thoughts, comments, and beliefs on YOUR life are only a reflection of THEIRS. It has everything to do with their own thoughts and triggers, of what they believe to be true, and zero to do with what is actually true for you. Most of the time, the people we take advice from don't even have the things we want or live the life that we want. Be careful who you choose to listen to.

There have been so many times in my life that I didn't have a person to look up to. I didn't know many people living life as an entrepreneur. I didn't know many people who had successfully moved away from my small little town. I didn't know many women who made more money than their male counterparts, and bought whatever the hell they wanted to because they thought they could. I didn't know many people who ran their own businesses on the Internet. I don't know many people who have written books or become authors. I have had strong, brilliant women around me and in my family for decades, and they have taught me a lot, but I haven't had many examples of people whose life I wanted to emulate.

However, if you wait around for an example of what to do next to get you where you want to go, you may not find one. If you take one thing from this book, it's that you are capable of anything that you want. You deserve to have a fulfilling life and all the crazy, obnoxious, shiny shit that goes with it. The only person standing in your way is the person in the mirror. Invest in yourself and in your mind, and you will be amazed at the places you will go. It is NEVER too late to reinvent yourself. I do it every day. Life can either be a wonderful, brilliant adventure, or it can suck balls. It's up to you, my love.

It's your decision to make.

Chapter 24:
Why Figuring Out Who You Are Is Bullsh*t

It drives me absolutely freakin' insane listening to people saying they need to figure out who they are, or what would make them happy, or if they are this type of person or that type of person. I used to be this way, too. Bullshit, bullshit, bullshit. You don't have to "figure out" who you are. You already know who you are. The person you are in this exact moment is exactly everything that you need to be to make your dreams come true. We just need to get you back in deeper communication with that person. Somewhere along the road, you got so used to silencing the voice that popped up and had dreams or told you what you wanted, that maybe you forgot how to listen to it. But, trust me, friend, it's there.

Who you are in this moment already IS exactly who you are supposed to be. You have every single thing inside of you that it takes to have the life that you want. Whatever job you are doing, the person you are with, the friends you have, they are all leading you to the person you will become. You are not the same as you were three years ago (or even three days ago), and you will not be the same person in another three months. You are constantly evolving and changing as a person. With that comes the need to sometimes let go of people, jobs, situations, and environments that no longer suit you. If you are consistently pissed off and upset, that is probably something that is no longer suiting you. So, it's up to you to have a conversation about it with that person, or, sometimes to just to let it fall away. No need for drama or a lengthy Facebook post. Just let it go.

I have reinvented myself plenty of times. I remember people commenting on my social media posts about my new ventures with "I thought you were doing X? What happened to that?" As if finding out something doesn't suit you and moving on to something else that does is not okay. I don't want to just do one thing for the rest of my life (except help others rock the shit out of their lives in some way, shape, or form), and chances are, neither do you.

Don't be afraid to change with what your soul calls to you. Complacency is close to death. Your time on this earth is short. LISTEN to that calling inside of you. Then, DO something about it. I *knew* I needed to leave H long before any of this mayhem happened. But I was comfortable and I wanted to avoid pain. I wish I'd had the courage to listen to the quiet voice inside of me that was calling for change. Don't hear that voice inside saying anything? Go to a quiet place. Sit in silence for a bit. Shut your stupid phone off and stop flipping through Instagram. Put your feet into the soil of the earth. Close your eyes and breathe. Repeat this process until you do start hearing something.

Once you decide to start listening to yourself (and that may take you a bit of time), give yourself permission to have what you desire. This one may sound simple, but it is actually the hardest part. I remember when I got pregnant, a girlfriend of mine told me (and I quote), "Get ready to give up a quality life." Meaning I'd have to give up trips, dreams, chances as an entrepreneur, adventures, lavish things like brand name clothing, you name it. I remember thinking to myself, WHY? Why can I not have a baby AND those things?

I believe that we (women especially) are so busy doing for others that we often don't do enough for ourselves. We lower our standards, we settle, we fall in line, so as not to be seen as too "needy," "bitchy," "selfish," "weak," you name it. Yet, ignoring the essence of who you are and what you deserve IS bitchy, selfish, needy, and weak. By avoiding what you are scared of being, you become it. It's okay to have everything you want. Disclaimer: This does not give you the right to treat people like shit and start taking the quiet, beautiful moments in life for granted. However, it does give you the right to start demanding more out of yourself and others.

I feel that I have only tapped into a small portion of who I am and what I can accomplish in life, and I hope to keep tapping into it. I hope I never stop changing and evolving, discovering, and uncovering.

Chapter 25:
Time Does Not Heal All Wounds. You Gotta Do the Work

They say that time heals all wounds, but it doesn't. Even if time heals the wounds, it will not heal the scars. The scars are important to pay attention to, because they are the things that stay with you long term. It's important to not let these scars wound you too deeply, to not let them affect who you want to be. I don't mean that you can't learn from them, that you can't make smarter decisions because of them, but don't let them change you for the worse.

A lot of times, we think sinking further into misery will hurt other people who have harmed us, but it doesn't. Those people only care about themselves. I know, it's sad but true. I hear women say this a lot after a man has hurt them—"I'm never dating a man again!" like you being alone and miserable your entire life will teach them. I know it makes sense right now, but in reality, it doesn't make any sense. You know what hurts other people? You giving yourself permission to live life to the fullest. To be who you really are. To show up and not take so much shit from others. To be caring and kind and compassionate. To know when to draw the line in the sand, when to stay, and when to keep it moving. That is what confuses and scares people (not that you should go around making decisions based on what people think—that is actually the opposite of the point I am trying to make).

Sometimes, when awful things happen, we need to feel like shit. In fact, this is me giving you 1,000% permission to feel awful for a while. Guess what? It totally sucks to be in pain, to be hurt, to be heartbroken, to feel loss. It's a real bitch (and not the kind you can be frenemies with later). Sometimes, we spend such a long time putting this part off, that we don't ever let the feelings sink in enough to be able to deal with them and move on. So, put on a *Real Housewives* marathon if you want. Don't get out of bed for a week (or maybe six). Eat leftover pizza with questionable expiration dates (at least you are eating something). Give yourself time to just be. I think that is the smartest thing you can do when horrible things happen.

After you throw yourself a pity party of the appropriate length (and only you can decide when that is—when you start to get sick of yourself, that is usually a sign you are ready to move on to the next phase), it's time to go in depth into what you want your life to be like. Go deep into who you are and what it is you want. Dream. Dream bigger. Then, dream some more. Just when you think you are dreaming too big, revisit it for an even grander dream. Only then have you gotten somewhere. Envision yourself being, doing, and having all the things. Close your eyes. Let it sink into your bones. Now the real work begins.

In order to get to that next level of you, you are going to have some hurt and pain and past scars to heal. In order to do that, you may have to hire someone. I'm not joking. A coach, a therapist, a psychic, a trusted friend, you name it. Sometimes, this journey is long and having help will shortcut it. Me personally? I hired a therapist, read books, journaled, exercised, meditated, did EFT tapping (highly recommend), did kinesthesia, invested in programs, asked for advice, did Reiki, got massages, did reflexology, even talked to a psychic. Want to laugh? Go for it. I was and am willing to do whatever it takes to be the best version of myself. When I finally hired a coach who spoke my language and who I understood, she helped me to understand that the me I am trying to become is here.

A friend of mine I used to complain about life with, suddenly stopped complaining. She started using transcendental language. Her body language shifted before my very eyes. I could see the light literally glowing inside of her. She started going for her dreams. She let go of drama. I reached out to her about a year and a half into my journey and said, "Dude, what are you doing?" She said to me, "I took this course from this lady. Here is her information. It really helped me change the way I looked at life in a huge way."

I reached out to the lady. I emailed her. I stalked her. When her course finally reopened, she let me know. I didn't care what it cost, I didn't care what she was teaching. From the words that she spoke and the information that she was doing, along with the shift I had seen in my friend, I just knew that I NEEDED her. Lo and behold, she became a mentor to me. The course at the time was way beyond my budget or what I was comfortable with paying. I envisioned myself as a CEO of my own business making millions of dollars a year. I put myself in that space and said, "Would that girl be afraid to invest in herself?" HELL TO THE NO she wouldn't be. So, I wouldn't be, either. I got out a credit card and I enrolled myself in her program. It worked for me. I made my investment back 10-fold so far.

This doesn't mean that YOU need to do exactly what I did or hire the same coach or mentor. The point is that you need to sometimes invest in yourself to make shifts. You can't do things the same way forever and expect different results. You have to start making decisions as if you were already reaching your big, wild goals. If someone speaks to you in your language or has what you want, invest in learning that information from them. It's a shortcut.

We can sometimes sabotage ourselves or become filled with emotional triggers, based on things that we haven't cleared deep down from our past. I always thought the past stuff was complete horse shit. I imagined a bunch of overgrown pussies sitting in a circle blaming their parents that they didn't get picked first for their adult softball league team. This is not what I am talking about at all. Simply uncovering some of the frustrations that you have, the reactions you have in life, and where exactly those came from, is the first step to healing them. When I started to heal those things, life changed dramatically for me.

You have to be willing to do the work—the hard work, the deep work, the emotional work. You must be willing to let go of some of the soap-opera-like drama you have become accustomed to. You have to separate yourself from the way you have always done things, and try something new. This is the only way you can get onto a new and better path. And, my friends, the new path holds nothing but opportunities for you.

I have never been afraid to walk the path less traveled, no matter who mocked me, or afraid to celebrate my failures, no matter who made fun of me or thought I was insane. And, armed with a new focus to live at a higher vibration, there is no telling what I will be able to create in this life (and hopefully this time I'll get it right, no conmen allowed).

Stop being afraid to fail.

Sometimes, you may try a job, a relationship, or a hobby and realize later on it's just not for you. You can call it failure, or you can recognize it as knowledge that you wouldn't have had before. Changing your mind isn't bad. Attempting something and realizing it isn't for you is NOT going backward, because you would have never known it if you hadn't gone that route. Sometimes, your biggest failures literally pave the path to what you were always supposed to be, do, and have anyway. Go for life with reckless abandon. Take action. Change your mind when you want. Stop doing shit if you realize it's not for you anymore. We talk ourselves into staying with stuff for OTHER people, when we are the only ones who pay the ultimate price. Only you are responsible for you at the end of the day, and where you end up. The time to try new things and change direction, to start that new thing or end that toxic relationship—is NOW.

Start being grateful for the lessons.

In fact, start being grateful in general. If you make it a daily habit to go through a gratitude list, you will be amazed how much your life will change. Even when things were at their lowest point, I'd at least be able to find some basics to be grateful for to get me through the day. Such as: I'm grateful for waking up, I'm grateful for my bed, I'm grateful for my health, I'm grateful for my family. I've heard it's best to do first thing in the morning, but just do it whenever and wherever you can. What have you got to lose?

You have to be extremely aware of the words that you use and your mindset. I have worked with some of today's leading entrepreneurs. I'm talking about people with multiple seven-figure businesses.

Do you want to know the difference between them and other people? They wholeheartedly believe they can have what they desire and aren't afraid to try. They work hard on their mindset, and so should you.

If you want all these positive "high vibration" things like joy, love, abundance, whatever that looks like for you, being negative and repeating lowly stuff will never reflect goodness into your life, because your life is a reflection of what you believe to be true. It's so important that I'm going to say it again. *Your life is a reflection of what you believe to be true.* Consciously and unconsciously. People will treat you in accordance with how you feel about yourself. Granted, sometimes people are just assholes. Yet, everyone is here to teach us something. Spend time working on your deep, emotional shit. Sure, it's not sexy, but your future is, and it will thank you for it.

Start spoiling yourself a little.

Do one thing each and every day that makes you feel good, and watch how your life shifts. It could be simple, like a walk outside or dancing to your favorite song. It could be eating your favorite candy bar (not 20, that will make you feel awful, duh), getting a massage, or watching your favorite trashy show. Think all this is crazy? So is doing the same thing over and over and expecting your life to be different. So, just try it, okay? Do it for me. But really, do it for you.

When you start mastering this, you will want to start outsourcing things that don't bring you joy when you are able to. What do I mean by this? One of my very successful clients hasn't done laundry in five years, hasn't washed a shirt, hasn't folded her pants, hasn't matched a sock. She hired someone to do this. Why? It's a small expense that takes something off her plate that brings her zero joy. She is blessing someone else's business by paying them to do it, and she gets that extra time each week to enjoy her family, take a walk outside, work on projects she loves, or do whatever brings her happiness.

Why are we so afraid to spend money, a renewable resource, for time, a non-renewable resource? You can make more money; you cannot make more time. This doesn't mean you should go into debt and live beyond your means, but once you prioritize yourself, shift your mindset, and raise your vibration, your life will shift. When it shifts financially enough for you to have a bit extra every week, don't be afraid to start spending some of it to buy your time back for yourself, okay?

What are you afraid of? Are you ready to start living (like REALLY living?) I hope so. I hope you will join me in this crazy dreamer's world where we can have a full life, creating magical things, surrounded by people who inspire and lift us up.

That is what I want for myself, and that is my parting wish for you.

Chapter 26:

Happy Endings?
(We're Not at a Massage Parlor)

*A*s I sit here in my kitchen writing this while sipping on some coffee, I realize how much life has changed for me. I have been through hard things, but haven't we all? Yet, as I stare at my partner and my little baby girl and I share these words with you, I cannot fathom the torture I put myself through to get here.

There is a state of flow in the world that feels so dang good when you can tap into it. These days look much different than they used to. I wake up and feed my daughter and go for a walk to hear the ocean. With the sun on my face, I look out as the waves crash and literally thank the heavens above that I am here, that I get to create and inspire, that I can write words hopefully that help other people. I get to be here for a lot of moments with my daughter. I get to enjoy a glass of wine with my friends on a nice patio and eat food that I love. Those things are blessings.

I have created courses and mentorship opportunities to allow others to build businesses and lives that they love. I get paid to be myself, kind of like a Kardashian (but not really). I have designed a life and business around things that suit me. What's next for me? I just really want to give back. I have created things for the woman that I was, for the things I was struggling with, for entrepreneurs who don't know what to do next or how to get where they want to be, for women who are stuck, for people who want to design a life of their dreams, too.

You can join our community of powerful people who are all about re-inventing themselves after hardships (or just because), building new lives and growing incredible businesses. We can support you if you're wanting to make shifts in life and to live on another level. We share the crazy shit, the tears, the laughter, all of it. We aren't afraid of failures. We give you the kick you need to get going with your dreams. And we pick you up when you don't know how to move forward. We are strong, resourceful, kind, compassionate, and sarcastic as hell, and we love fiercely. We also like to have FUN.

If these are the kind of women you want to surround yourself with, join the free community here:

www.danielleprahl.com/party

If you want to know more about me or what I do, you can find me hanging out online here:

www.danielleprahl.com

Thank you for taking your valuable time to share in my stories, adventures, lessons and dreams. Let's change the world together.

xx.

Danielle

www.ingramcontent.com/pod-product-compliance
Lightning Source LLC
Chambersburg PA
CBHW060021100426
42740CB00010B/1557